What are people saying about
The Gospel of Ruth?

In her gutsy profile of biblical Ruth, Carolyn Custis James challenges old religious mind-sets about gender, how God uses women, and how men should respond to the Holy Spirit's work in women. *The Gospel of Ruth* is one of the richest and most insightful books I've ever read about any woman in the Bible. Carolyn is to be commended for making such a valuable contribution to biblical theology.

J. Lee Grady
author of *10 Lies the Church Tells Women*

Writing in an engaging and winsome style, Carolyn Custis James considers the intriguing question, "Is God good for women?" through an in-depth study of the book of Ruth. Women who want to live for Christ will appreciate her critique of the biblical concept of submission in light of the gospel. But don't leave the men out! They, too, will better understand what it means to be a Christian man through her solidly Christian discussion of male-female relationships in Christ.

Karen H. Jobes, PhD
Gerald F. Hawthorne Professor of New Testament Greek
and Exegesis, Wheaton College

The Gospel of Ruth sparkles with cultural insights and contemporary illustrations that bring the biblical story of Ruth into direct contact with the lives of women in the twenty-first century.

Robert H. Gundry
scholar-in-residence and professor emeritus, Westmont College,
Santa Barbara, California

Carolyn Custis James refuses to reduce Ruth to a pretty story with a nice moral lesson. Instead, she makes this ancient woman of faith come alive for women — and men — today. A work of theological insight and practical Christian wisdom.

Timothy George
founding dean of Beeson Divinity School of Samford University
and a senior editor of *Christianity Today*

The Gospel of Ruth is indeed Good News as Carolyn Custis James writes compellingly of the essential importance of women—and men—in God's redemptive plan.

Carla Foote
editor of *FullFill* magazine

Carolyn James reinterprets the story of Naomi and Ruth from a romance novel into what its author intended: life-transforming, character-building biographies. This is so because Carolyn allows the harsh fate and profound love rooted in faith of these gutsy women to interpret her own narrative of trials trumped by her trust in God's sovereignty, goodness, and love.

Bruce Waltke
professor of Old Testament, Reformed Theological Seminary (Orlando) and Professor Emeritus of Biblical Studies, Regent College

This surprising examination of Ruth reveals so much more treasure than we thought this book held—reminding us of God's presence and work in troubled times.

Amy Simpson
executive director, Leadership Media Group,
Christianity Today International

Carolyn James provides a compelling and riveting reading of the book of Ruth that reveals its grace-full message and will change your assumptions about Ruth as well as Naomi and Boaz. Even more, this book will challenge your preconceptions about the relationships between men and women. I strongly encourage women and men to read this book.

Tremper Longman, III
Robert H. Gundry Professor of Biblical Studies,
Westmont College

Carolyn Custis James' journey through Ruth breathed courage into me, to show me that I am most feminine when I own the gifts God has given me, when I partner with my brothers in Christ, when I trust Ruth's example that when strong men meet strong women, both masculinity and femininity become mightier. I want to be like Ruth, a woman who lived in bold, innovative, risky love of Yahweh, a woman who encountered a strong Boaz and coupled her mind with his to show the world more of what God is like. *The Gospel of Ruth* will remind you that God is stunningly good for women.

Jonalyn Grace Fincher
author, apologist, and speaker

Carolyn James has made the story of Ruth come alive in new ways for women — and for men! — who live in today's complex and confusing world. This is a marvelous book that offers much wisdom and inspiration for all of us.

Richard J. Mouw
president and professor of Christian philosophy,
Fuller Theological Seminary

I have not read (nor, I expect, have you) a more discerning, humbling, thought-provoking, God-honoring, life-enhancing treatment of Ruth than this one. It makes an outstandingly fruitful study for believers of all ages and both genders.

J. I. Packer
professor of theology, Regent College

This is not a woman's book ... it is a powerful book that I wish every man and woman who call themselves Christian would read. Carolyn Custis James peels back the familiar story of Ruth and shows us the undeniable story of courage, equality, and partnership that reflect the gospel and that the world is hungry to see.

Nancy Ortberg
author of *LookingforGod*;
founding partner, Teamworx2

Also by Carolyn Custis James

Lost Women of the Bible
When Life and Beliefs Collide

THE GOSPEL OF
Ruth

Loving God Enough to
Break the Rules

CAROLYN
CUSTIS JAMES

ZONDERVAN

ZONDERVAN.com/
AUTHORTRACKER
follow your favorite authors

We want to hear from you. Please send your comments about this book to us in care of zreview@zondervan.com. Thank you.

ZONDERVAN

The Gospel of Ruth
Copyright © 2008 by Carolyn Custis James

This title is also available as a Zondervan ebook.
Visit www.zondervan.com/ebooks.

This title is also available in a Zondervan audio edition.
Visit www.zondervan.fm.

Requests for information should be addressed to:

Zondervan, *Grand Rapids, Michigan 49530*

This edition: ISBN 978-0-310-33085-1 (softcover)

Library of Congress Cataloging-in-Publication Data

James, Carolyn Custis.
    The gospel of Ruth : loving God enough to break the rules / Carolyn Custis James.
        p. cm.
    Includes bibliographical references.
    ISBN 978-0-310-26391-3 (hardcover)
    1. Bible. O.T. Ruth—Criticism, interpretation, etc. I. Title.
BS1315.53.J36 2007
222'.3506—dc22   2007032253

Published in association with the literary agency of Wolgemuth Associates, Inc.

Cover design: Rob Monacelli
Cover photography: Tamara Reynolds / Getty Images
Interior design: Melissa Elenbaas

Printed in the United States of America

---

13 14 15 16 17 18 19 /DCI/ 22 21 20 19 18 17 16 15 14 13 12 11 10 9 8 7 6 5 4 3

Dedicated with love
to my husband, Frank.

Like Boaz,
you are a man who gets it.
You've listened, partnered, advocated,
and
(when I needed it)
given me a push.
You've valued me and my gifts,
opened doors of opportunity I thought were stuck shut,
then sacrificed, coached, and cheered me on.
My world is bigger because of you.
This book (and all the others)
wouldn't exist without you.

Contents

FOREWORD

So, you've decided to read *The Gospel of Ruth* by Carolyn Custis James. Let me tell you upfront: you're in for a very rich feast! She's spread a deliciously full biblical banquet table for you to enjoy. You will not be disappointed. If you're a woman, stand by for some very, very good news. If you're a man, prepare to enter a woman's world. You may find it surprising and strange, but listen and learn anyway.

Carolyn Custis James brings to life for today the book of Ruth, a book written long ago and far away. That is no easy task. "The past," as someone once said, "is a very different place; they do things differently there." To write a book about Ruth requires an author to live with women in two very different worlds. She must live in the ancient world of Moab and Bethlehem. That is a world without cars and computers, without electricity and email, without refrigerators and radios. Sunrise is the alarm clock that starts the day, sunset the signal to go home at night. At night city streets are empty and dark, and families share evenings by candle-light. Food comes directly from fields and orchards. Milk is hand-wrung daily from goats that hang around the house. People prepare meals from scratch. And by hand. And one meal at a time.

The ancient world is also a world run by men, so life for women is tricky. The work is hard, but the pace of life leisurely. A widow can remarry, but only to a relative of her late husband. And every-one speaks Hebrew. Back there, "they do things differently."

The author must also live in the modern world of her readers. There, a clock radio wakes them up before or after sunrise, and sunset doesn't necessarily send them home. At night the city streets are well-lit and busy, and families flip a switch to light the evening. Somewhere nearby a TV screen flickers and speakers pour out sounds. People rarely visit fields or orchards. Their milk comes in cartons, their contents machine-wrung from cows many miles out of sight. They buy food in boxes and cans from supermarket shelves. They prepare meals by heating—using electricity or gas—the stuff inside those boxes and cans. Or leftovers from meals days ago.

The world is run by women and men, but life for a woman remains tricky. The work is easy, but the pace of life frenetic. A widow can marry anyone she wants, but she's on her own in finding someone. And people speak Spanish, Polish, Korean, Navajo, Chinese, Italian, and regional dialects of English. And they all live in the same country—and often in the same city!

In *The Gospel of Ruth* Carolyn Custis James has succeeded on all counts. She's a reliable guide to the ancient world of Ruth and to the modern world of women. She knows the issues that trouble women today, including women outside North America. She skillfully leads the reader through the book of Ruth, letting women hear its "good news" for them in a powerful voice. In her expert hands, the biblical characters come alive in flesh, blood, and texture beyond the stereotypes of a nice love story.

She also carefully tracks God's role in this biblical book and unpacks how he relates to Naomi, Ruth, and Boaz. With keen insight, she draws important implications from their relationship for life with God today. It all adds up to good news for women. That in itself marks a bold claim, especially for an Old Testament book. But, as I see it, she's absolutely right.

So, you've decided to read *The Gospel of Ruth* by Carolyn Custis James. Excellent! I guarantee that you won't be sorry. Her engaging writing, insightful commentary, and winsome spirit bring its message and implications vividly to life. Turn the page and start a wonderful journey. Above all, prepare to hear and believe "the Gospel of Ruth."

Robert L. Hubbard Jr.
Professor of Old Testament, North Park Theological Seminary, Chicago; general editor of New International Commentary on the Old Testament

PREFACE

This is the book I was born to write. I've often heard aspiring writers talk about that one book churning inside them that they can't wait to get out. *The Gospel of Ruth* is that book for me.

Several years ago, Old Testament scholars began to think differently about the book of Ruth. A Bible story I thought I knew as well as my own name emerged from the fringes of biblical literature into the spotlight—contributing substantially to our understanding of God and giving a picture of how he means for his sons and daughters to build his kingdom together. The book of Ruth opened up a whole new world of possibilities for me.

Never have I been more surprised, never more strongly impacted, never more redirected than I was by being reintroduced to Naomi, Ruth, and Boaz. The message of the book was so revolutionary, so life-changing, so unlike what I had always been taught, I knew I couldn't keep it to myself.

Yet, for one reason or another, this project kept getting set aside for others that, in hindsight, I now see needed to come first. The payoff for the delay has been the added time it has given me to drill down deeper, probe, and ponder Ruth for myself. After simmering on this book for years, I have a great deal more to say than if I had written *The Gospel of Ruth* earlier.

For a long, long time we've all been looking at the lives of Naomi and Ruth (as well as other women in the Bible) through the wrong end of the telescope. Their lives have all too often been diminished in size, noticeably small next to the larger lives of the men in their stories. This has influenced how we see ourselves.

Even when Ruth does something remarkable and brave, evangelicals have tended to turn her story into a romance and Boaz into the hero who comes to her rescue. Nothing could be further from the truth.

I never will forget the day someone turned the telescope around for me and I saw Naomi and Ruth in truer perspective. I wept to think of how much more I could have (should have) done and was indeed called by God to do with my life. Life-sized at last, Ruth became for me the most powerful and challenging role model I've yet to encounter in the Bible. During the losses and heartaches that have come my way through the writing of this book, I have found Naomi to be a wise mentor, a comfort, and a hopeful counselor. I would hate to have lived through this past year of writing without her.

The book opens by clearing the stage of all male characters—not to establish notions of female superiority as some might wish, but to give us a clear view of the women and underscore the fact that the story centers on them and on their relationships with God. It sets the stage for us to see the Bible's unrivaled regard for women (no other viewpoint comes close) and the kind of strong alliance between men and women God intended from creation.

Although much of a writer's life is spent in solitude—studying, reflecting, hammering out chapters at the computer—in a real sense, this book was written in a community, for which I am deeply grateful.

My husband Frank is always my strongest advocate and toughest editor. As I've cranked out chapters, he and I have enjoyed some unforgettable conversations about Naomi, Ruth, and Boaz. Four trusted friends—Susan Anders, Milli Jacks, Dixie Fraley Keller, and Alexis McElhinney—have accompanied me every step of the way, reading chapters, giving me thoughtful feedback and encouragement to keep me going. I am also thankful for relatives and friends who have prayed, supported, and listened along the way. Foremost among them are my parents, Dwight and Lucille Custis, and my cousin, Karen Custis Wilson, who are always just a phone call or an email away.

Special thanks to Robert, Andrew, and Erik Wolgemuth, who are always looking out for me and cheering me on. I'm blessed to have you in my corner!

Thanks to my friends at Zondervan: Stan Gundry, who has mentored and supported me from the beginning of my writing career; Katya Covrett, a kindred spirit and a relentless advocate; Verlyn Verbrugge, whose expert editing made this a better book; John Topliff, for helping me reach a wider audience with this message; Rob Monacelli, for designing the perfect jacket; and Mark Sheeres, for the internal layout.

Thanks also to the library staff of Reformed Theological Seminary/Orlando—Keely Leim, Karen Middlesworth, and Michael Farrell—who assisted my research.

I am especially indebted to Robert L. Hubbard Jr., Katharine Doob Sakenfeld, Edward F. Campbell Jr., Frederic Bush, Bruce K. Waltke, and Ellen Davis. Their scholarly efforts launched my own study and gave me courage to dig even deeper into this ancient book of the Bible and engage the biblical text with questions I and so many other women are asking today.

And now at last the book is finished, and you are holding it in your hands. I hope you are as eager to begin reading as I am to begin telling you about *The Gospel of Ruth*.

NIV Text of Ruth

Naomi and Ruth

1 In the days when the judges ruled, there was a famine in the land, and a man from Bethlehem in Judah, together with his wife and two sons, went to live for a while in the country of Moab. ²The man's name was Elimelech, his wife's name Naomi, and the names of his two sons were Mahlon and Kilion. They were Ephrathites from Bethlehem, Judah. And they went to Moab and lived there.

³Now Elimelech, Naomi's husband, died, and she was left with her two sons. ⁴They married Moabite women, one named Orpah and the other Ruth. After they had lived there about ten years, ⁵both Mahlon and Kilion also died, and Naomi was left without her two sons and her husband.

⁶When she heard in Moab that the LORD had come to the aid of his people by providing food for them, Naomi and her daughters-in-law prepared to return home from there. ⁷With her two daughters-in-law she left the place where she had been living and set out on the road that would take them back to the land of Judah.

⁸Then Naomi said to her two daughters-in-law, "Go back, each of you, to your mother's home. May the LORD show kindness [*hesed*] to you, as you have shown to your dead and to me. ⁹May the LORD grant that each of you will find rest in the home of another husband."

Then she kissed them and they wept aloud ¹⁰and said to her, "We will go back with you to your people."

¹¹But Naomi said, "Return home, my daughters. Why would you come with me? Am I going to have any more sons, who could become your husbands? ¹²Return home, my daughters; I am too old to have another husband. Even if I thought there was still hope for me—even if I had a husband tonight and then gave birth to sons—¹³would you wait until they grew up? Would you remain unmarried for them? No, my daughters. It is more bitter for me than for you, because the LORD's hand has gone out against me!"

¹⁴At this they wept again. Then Orpah kissed her mother-in-law good-by, but Ruth clung to her.

¹⁵"Look," said Naomi, "your sister-in-law is going back to her people and her gods. Go back with her."

¹⁶But Ruth replied, "Don't urge me to leave you or to turn back from you. Where you go I will go, and where you stay I will stay. Your people will be my people and your God my God. ¹⁷Where you die I will die, and there I will be buried. May the LORD deal with me, be it ever so severely, if anything but death separates you and me." ¹⁸When Naomi realized that Ruth was determined to go with her, she stopped urging her.

¹⁹So the two women went on until they came to Bethlehem. When they arrived in Bethlehem, the whole town was stirred because of them, and the women exclaimed, "Can this be Naomi?"

²⁰"Don't call me Naomi," she told them. "Call me Mara, because the Almighty has made my life very bitter. ²¹I went away full, but the LORD has brought me back empty. Why call me Naomi? The LORD has afflicted me; the Almighty has brought misfortune upon me."

²²So Naomi returned from Moab accompanied by Ruth the Moabitess, her daughter-in-law, arriving in Bethlehem as the barley harvest was beginning.

Ruth Meets Boaz

2 Now Naomi had a relative on her husband's side, from the clan of Elimelech, a man of standing [*hayil*], whose name was Boaz.

²And Ruth the Moabitess said to Naomi, "Let me go to the fields and pick up the leftover grain behind anyone in whose eyes I find favor."

Naomi said to her, "Go ahead, my daughter." ³So she went out and began to glean in the fields behind the harvesters. As it turned out, she found herself working in a field belonging to Boaz, who was from the clan of Elimelech.

⁴Just then Boaz arrived from Bethlehem and greeted the harvesters, "The Lord be with you! "

"The Lord bless you!" they called back.

⁵Boaz asked the foreman of his harvesters, "Whose young woman is that?"

⁶The foreman replied, "She is the Moabitess who came back from Moab with Naomi. ⁷She said, 'Please let me glean and gather among the sheaves behind the harvesters.' She went into the field and has worked steadily from morning till now, except for a short rest in the shelter."

⁸So Boaz said to Ruth, "My daughter, listen to me. Don't go and glean in another field and don't go away from here. Stay here with my servant girls. ⁹Watch the field where the men are harvesting, and follow along after the girls. I have told the men not to touch you. And whenever you are thirsty, go and get a drink from the water jars the men have filled."

¹⁰At this, she bowed down with her face to the ground. She exclaimed, "Why have I found such favor in your eyes that you notice me—a foreigner?"

¹¹Boaz replied, "I've been told all about what you have done for your mother-in-law since the death of your husband—how you left your father and mother and your homeland and came to live with a people you did not know before. ¹²May the Lord repay you for what you have done. May you be richly rewarded by the Lord, the God of Israel, under whose wings you have come to take refuge."

¹³"May I continue to find favor in your eyes, my lord," she said. "You have given me comfort and have spoken kindly to your servant—though I do not have the standing of one of your servant girls."

^{14}At mealtime Boaz said to her, "Come over here. Have some bread and dip it in the wine vinegar."

When she sat down with the harvesters, he offered her some roasted grain. She ate all she wanted and had some left over. ^{15}As she got up to glean, Boaz gave orders to his men, "Even if she gathers among the sheaves, don't embarrass her. ^{16}Rather, pull out some stalks for her from the bundles and leave them for her to pick up, and don't rebuke her."

^{17}So Ruth gleaned in the field until evening. Then she threshed the barley she had gathered, and it amounted to about an ephah. ^{18}She carried it back to town, and her mother-in-law saw how much she had gathered. Ruth also brought out and gave her what she had left over after she had eaten enough.

^{19}Her mother-in-law asked her, "Where did you glean today? Where did you work? Blessed be the man who took notice of you!"

Then Ruth told her mother-in-law about the one at whose place she had been working. "The name of the man I worked with today is Boaz," she said.

^{20}"The LORD bless him!" Naomi said to her daughter-in-law. "He has not stopped showing his kindness [*hesed*] to the living and the dead." She added, "That man is our close relative; he is one of our kinsman-redeemers [*go'el*]."

^{21}Then Ruth the Moabitess said, "He even said to me, 'Stay with my workers until they finish harvesting all my grain.'"

^{22}Naomi said to Ruth her daughter-in-law, "It will be good for you, my daughter, to go with his girls, because in someone else's field you might be harmed."

^{23}So Ruth stayed close to the servant girls of Boaz to glean until the barley and wheat harvests were finished. And she lived with her mother-in-law.

Ruth and Boaz at the Threshing Floor

3 One day Naomi her mother-in-law said to her, "My daughter, should I not try to find a home for you, where you will be well provided for? ^{2}Is not Boaz, with whose servant girls you have been, a kinsman of ours? Tonight he will be winnowing barley on the threshing floor. ³Wash and perfume yourself, and put on your best clothes. Then go down to the threshing floor, but don't let him know you are there until he has finished eating and drinking. ⁴When he lies down, note the place where he is lying. Then go and uncover his feet and lie down. He will tell you what to do."

⁵"I will do whatever you say," Ruth answered. ⁶So she went down to the threshing floor and did everything her mother-in-law told her to do.

⁷When Boaz had finished eating and drinking and was in good spirits, he went over to lie down at the far end of the grain pile. Ruth approached quietly, uncovered his feet and lay down. ⁸In the middle of the night something startled the man, and he turned and discovered a woman lying at his feet.

⁹"Who are you?" he asked.

"I am your servant Ruth," she said. "Spread the corner of your garment over me, since you are a kinsman-redeemer [go'el]."

¹⁰"The LORD bless you, my daughter," he replied. "This kindness [hesed] is greater than that which you showed earlier: You have not run after the younger men, whether rich or poor. ¹¹And now, my daughter, don't be afraid. I will do for you all you ask. All my fellow townsmen know that you are a woman of noble character [hayil]. ¹²Although it is true that I am near of kin [go'el], there is a kinsman-redeemer [go'el] nearer than I. ¹³Stay here for the night, and in the morning if he wants to redeem, good; let him redeem. But if he is not willing, as surely as the LORD lives I will do it. Lie here until morning."

¹⁴So she lay at his feet until morning, but got up before anyone could be recognized; and he said, "Don't let it be known that a woman came to the threshing floor."

¹⁵He also said, "Bring me the shawl you are wearing and hold it out." When she did so, he poured into it six measures of barley and put it on her. Then he went back to town.

¹⁶When Ruth came to her mother-in-law, Naomi asked, "How did it go, my daughter?"

Then she told her everything Boaz had done for her [17]and added, "He gave me these six measures of barley, saying, 'Don't go back to your mother-in-law empty-handed.'"

[18]Then Naomi said, "Wait, my daughter, until you find out what happens. For the man will not rest until the matter is settled today."

Boaz Marries Ruth

4 Meanwhile Boaz went up to the town gate and sat there. When the kinsman-redeemer [go'el] he had mentioned came along, Boaz said, "Come over here, my friend, and sit down." So he went over and sat down.

[2]Boaz took ten of the elders of the town and said, "Sit here," and they did so. [3]Then he said to the kinsman-redeemer [go'el], "Naomi, who has come back from Moab, is selling the piece of land that belonged to our brother Elimelech. [4]I thought I should bring the matter to your attention and suggest that you buy it in the presence of these seated here and in the presence of the elders of my people. If you will redeem it, do so. But if you will not, tell me, so I will know. For no one has the right to do it except you, and I am next in line."

"I will redeem it," he said.

[5]Then Boaz said, "On the day you buy the land from Naomi and from Ruth the Moabitess, you acquire the dead man's widow, in order to maintain the name of the dead with his property."

[6]At this, the kinsman-redeemer [go'el] said, "Then I cannot redeem it because I might endanger my own estate. You redeem it yourself. I cannot do it."

[7](Now in earlier times in Israel, for the redemption and transfer of property to become final, one party took off his sandal and gave it to the other. This was the method of legalizing transactions in Israel.)

[8]So the kinsman-redeemer [go'el] said to Boaz, "Buy it yourself." And he removed his sandal.

[9]Then Boaz announced to the elders and all the people, "Today you are witnesses that I have bought from Naomi all the property of Elimelech, Kilion and Mahlon. [10]I have also acquired Ruth the Moabitess, Mahlon's widow, as my wife, in

order to maintain the name of the dead with his property, so that his name will not disappear from among his family or from the town records. Today you are witnesses!"

¹¹Then the elders and all those at the gate said, "We are witnesses. May the LORD make the woman who is coming into your home like Rachel and Leah, who together built up the house of Israel. May you have standing in Ephrathah and be famous in Bethlehem. ¹²Through the offspring the LORD gives you by this young woman, may your family be like that of Perez, whom Tamar bore to Judah."

The Genealogy of David

¹³So Boaz took Ruth and she became his wife. Then he went to her, and the LORD enabled her to conceive, and she gave birth to a son. ¹⁴The women said to Naomi: "Praise be to the LORD, who this day has not left you without a kinsman-redeemer [go'el]. May he become famous throughout Israel! ¹⁵He will renew your life and sustain you in your old age. For your daughter-in-law, who loves you and who is better to you than seven sons, has given him birth."

¹⁶Then Naomi took the child, laid him in her lap and cared for him. ¹⁷The women living there said, "Naomi has a son." And they named him Obed. He was the father of Jesse, the father of David.

¹⁸This, then, is the family line of Perez:

Perez was the father of Hezron,

¹⁹Hezron the father of Ram,

Ram the father of Amminadab,

²⁰Amminadab the father of Nahshon,

Nahshon the father of Salmon,

²¹Salmon the father of Boaz,

Boaz the father of Obed,

²²Obed the father of Jesse,

and Jesse the father of David.

Introduction

WHAT WOMEN WANT TO KNOW

Is God good for women?

The question emblazed on the jacket of the book I was holding caught my attention and made me want to drop what I was doing and lose myself in a good read. I was intrigued because, for one thing, the way it fell into my hands was something of a miracle. But there was a second, even stronger reason why I didn't want to put this one down.

It was summer in Oxford. My family had returned to England principally on business, but also to enjoy again this old city and the people there whom we had come to love and who commanded such a big part of our family history. My husband, Frank, was teaching summer school at the Centre for Medieval and Renaissance Studies. Our daughter, Allison, was brushing up on her British vocabulary and refreshing early childhood memories of England. I was checking on Oxford clients for my computer software business. On a personal level, I was also swerving around one of those sharp bends in the road that are so common to a woman's journey and that at least in part sparked my sudden interest in the book.

Miracle in Blackwell's Bookstore

The miracle had to do with my husband. After delivering his morning lectures, Frank left the Centre, hurried along Oxford's narrow back alleyways, and turned onto historic Broad Street, which by now was swarming with tourists and traffic. A block or two of crowded sidewalk, noise, and exhaust fumes brought him to his destination. Leaving the hubbub behind, he shoved open the door and disappeared into the quiet serenity of Blackwell's Bookstore. Friends who were traveling in the UK (and were unaware of the threat this might pose to our family budget) had arranged to meet him in this book lover's paradise, arguably one of the best bookstores in the world. As it turned out, he was thirty minutes early, and they were running late. So while Oxford and I went blithely about our business, my husband was savoring a leisurely browse through endless rows of books with a credit card at his fingertips.

Few people would be able to withstand the force of such temptation. If you have ever known or happen to be a person with a passion for books, you will understand. But miracles still happen, and nearly two hours later my husband reemerged from the bookstore with a single book tucked under his arm, the book I now held in my hands, which he had purchased for me.

That miracle alone would have been enough to excite my interest in the book. But the question posed in bold letters on the jacket intrigued me even more. *Is God good for women?* Here was a question that had quietly nagged at me for years and was resurfacing in the changes I was experiencing at the moment.

Life after Oxford

During our Oxford years, when my husband was in doctoral studies, I formed mental pictures of what life after Oxford would be like and longed for that day to come. Once his D.Phil. was firmly in hand and we were stateside again, we settled our daughter in school, bought a house, found a church, and put down roots. Everything was going according to plan. What caught me off guard, however, was the fact that this eagerly awaited phase brought a sense of loss to me that triggered a whole new wave of soul searching I had not anticipated. Post-Oxford, I entered a new period of reflection and discovery—about God, about myself, and about God's mission for his daughters in the world.

Perhaps the most significant change (one we expected and actually aimed for) was that for the first time in our marriage I was no longer the main breadwinner. My work, which had been our bread and butter during seminary and in Oxford, was no longer what was keeping us financially afloat. While helpful to our family, my income wasn't essential anymore.

This wasn't the first time (or the last) that my circumstances would unsettle me and stir up misgivings about where I fit into God's purposes. Did I still have important contributions to make? I wondered if God, in any sense, was counting on me to build his kingdom, or if it was enough for me to help launch Frank to do important kingdom work. Were my efforts now less important—-even dispensable—because I am a woman?

At one level, my callings as a wife and a mother were deeply satisfying. But my daughter was growing up, and I could see my days of mothering were numbered. Furthermore, my husband, while believing that his work and mine were deeply intertwined, never believed his profession was the answer to questions I was asking about God's calling for me. So did I have a calling?

The book Frank bought for me was a timely reminder that I wasn't the only woman wrestling with such questions. In fact, these are actually old questions that have resurfaced in women's lives during every generation. In no time, I was poring over the pages of my new book to see how British women from a variety of backgrounds and professions answered the question, "Is God good for women?"

IN GOOD COMPANY

The women I met inside the book all faced situations that caused them to question God's goodness to women. Remarkably, as they made their way in a man's world, their struggles and the obstacles they encountered didn't embitter them or hold them back. The firm conviction that God is good for women fueled their courage and freed them to invest their energies to fight the battles he called them to engage in. In the end, God used them to make a difference in a lot of lives.

One woman founded the first European hospice for AIDS sufferers, ministering to patients and grieving family members and (when opportunity presented) giving the gospel. A police superintendent, after witnessing appalling crimes on the beat, used her clout as a high-ranking police officer to influence British politicians to enact laws improving the treatment of victims of rape and domestic violence. One of the twelve started a fashion consultancy to design and make well-fitting, easy-to-manage, stylish clothing for disabled people that gave them greater independence and lifted their spirits.

Their efforts made the world a better place for a lot of people and painted a larger picture for me of the big things God is doing through his daughters today. Yet, although their conclusions about God were encouraging, the consensus of twelve or even twelve thousand women about God's goodness, while offering hope, in the final analysis, simply wasn't enough. To rest on opinions in matters of such gravity left me dangling in a wind of changing circumstances that too easily could blow one way today and the opposite way tomorrow. I needed something more.

The real breakthrough in my thinking came when I discovered that the Bible has a lot to say on the subject of God's goodness to women. In fact, this ancient book treats the subject openly and with surprising candor. Suddenly I had my finger on a biblical text where God's love comes under fire within the context of women's lives. Remarkably, he not only affirms his love for his daughters in radical and earthshaking ways, he does so within a patriarchal culture that unapologetically relegated women to second-class status. What is more, against that backdrop, God casts a vision of breathtaking proportions for how his kingdom is moving forward through the efforts of women—*ordinary* women like most of us. I found the good news (gospel) I was looking for in the Old Testament book of Ruth.

A New Day for Naomi

If you had asked me earlier that year whether I understood the message of Ruth, I would have answered without the slightest hesitation that I did. After all, I had heard this story all my life and had even taught it several times. That was before my friend Dr. Bruce Waltke tipped me off that Old Testament scholars are still digging around and breaking new ground in their understanding of this beloved story. What I would learn from them galvanized my own study of Ruth and opened up a whole new horizon of possibilities for how a woman can invest her life as a follower of Jesus.

After that, at every opportunity, I was delving into commentaries to find out what scholars were discovering. I know it sounds a bit strange, but these books were real page-turners for me. Once during dinner, my husband (who was watching the evening news) was highly amused when he caught me secretly reading snatches from Robert Hubbard's thick commentary on Ruth,[1] which I had propped on my lap under the table. The book of Ruth was coming alive for me in ways I never imagined and that surprised me in its relevance to the kinds of issues Christian women are facing today.

First came a sobering dose of humility, for it was clear I didn't (and still don't) know as much as I thought about a book of the Bible I had studied a lot. At the same time, this was a joyous awakening to the fact that no matter how much we've learned about the Bible, there is always more — much more — to discover. Even scholars have only scratched the surface of what there is to learn about God through his Word. So, with the help of God's Spirit, our reading and studying of God's Word always holds the promise of greater discovery and learning for all of us.

Several factors utterly changed the book of Ruth for me. First, I learned that the Ruth story is told from Naomi's point of view. The narrator writes of Naomi's husband, her sons, her daughters-in-law, her losses, her God, her return to Bethlehem, her people, her relative, and the land she is selling. Readers are observing events as they relate to her. We also view God through the eyes of a woman.

The book gives us the saga of two women on their own in a patriarchal culture. The narrator tracks their amazing struggle to survive against all odds in the workplace, the community of God's people, and the legal system. As we might expect, the story is loaded with feminine themes. Widowhood and marriage, barrenness and childbirth, single parenting, loss of a child, the caregiver, and male/female relationships all come up.

The second major development relates to Naomi herself. At the hands of leading evangelical scholars, she has undergone something of a makeover—not to conceal blemishes or dress up her appearance, but to unveil Naomi in her true colors and to restore her dignity. First to go was her former reputation as a bitter, complaining old woman. Once widely dismissed by Christians as out-of-sorts, Naomi has been upgraded from a self-absorbed malcontent to the full stature of a female Job.[2] Parallels between the two sufferers (which we will explore in chapter 1) are striking. The extent of their losses, their agonized bewilderment and wrestlings with God, even their bitter laments are mirror images of each other. Yet historically, we have wept with Job and criticized Naomi. No more, say Old Testament scholars. Now we will weep with Naomi too.

Naomi in her own way is properly identified as a theologian, for the centerpiece of her story is her quest to know and walk with God. Her voice belongs in the arena of deep theological discussion, where she has much to offer. No longer can we regard Ruth as a lightweight among the deeper books of the Bible. This is not some sweet romantic interlude tucked in among the more significant prophetic and historical writings to relieve the tension generated by sordid accounts of God's people in moral decline. The book stands on its own as a substantial contribution to our understanding of God.

The implications of this development are utterly profound for us, for in Naomi's story a woman's questions about God are raised to the highest level of significance. "Is God good for women?" and "Has my usefulness expired?" are no longer private matters for women to sort out on their own. These are vital biblical issues that the book of Ruth highlights for the contemplation and enlightenment of all of God's people—both women and men.

Naomi's story is a gift to the church, for it gives us another opportunity to talk honestly about our own misgivings about God and to witness how a woman's life is transformed by the discovery that God's love for her is rock solid, even though her circumstances indicate otherwise. But Naomi isn't the only one to benefit from recent advances in biblical research. Her Moabite daughter-in-law has improved under closer inspection as well.

Taking Another Look at Ruth

Careful reexamination of the Hebrew text has effectively removed the shrink-wrap that for generations has encased Ruth. She emerges, not as the passive, deferential, demure woman we once thought we knew, but as a surprisingly gutsy risk taker. The young Moabite widow discards cultural protocol, her own hopes of happiness, and even plain reason when she embraces Naomi's terrifying God and binds herself for life to her mother-in-law. In one pivotal moment, Ruth's identity and center of gravity change forever. The rest of her story is a stunning (and at times shocking) chronicle of her efforts to live out what it means to be Yahweh's child.

Her bold initiatives have all Bethlehem talking. In her case, local gossip is a good thing, for it brings universal admiration to this unpredictable immigrant from Moab. Her loyalty to Yahweh prompts her to challenge the religious status quo and lead others into a whole new realm of allegiance to Yahweh that carries early hints of the teachings of Jesus. I will go so far as to say that Ruth herself embodies the utter difference the gospel makes in us and in our relationships with others—generations *before* Jesus was born. We definitely need to take another look at this "Gospel of Ruth."

But what about Boaz, you may ask? What does Boaz lose?

Benefits for Boaz

I once asked a seminary professor if he saw a pattern in the biblical text where men interacting with strong women became stronger themselves. I'll never forget the blank look I got in return. In Christian circles, there is sometimes an assumption that when women step into the spotlight, the men will pay a price. The spotlight of recent research may train its sights on Naomi and Ruth, but until now this beam of light belonged to Boaz, the Kinsman-Redeemer Christ figure, traditionally identified as the hero of the story. Introduced into the narrative as a man of valor, Boaz has a lot to lose. Yet amazingly, even with two strong women in his life, there are no blank stares coming from Boaz.

Though this may come as a surprise to some, even Boaz gains significantly. He is Exhibit A for the pattern I was asking my seminary professor about, for Boaz is not diminished, marginalized, or feminized in the slightest by being outnumbered and influenced by Ruth and Naomi. As a matter of fact, he only grows stronger himself through his collaborations with them. If anything, previous characterizations of Boaz as the "romantic lead" in this narrative have actually detracted from his true significance and cheated him of the enormous credit he truly deserves. But, I'm getting ahead of myself. For now, suffice it to say, that Boaz loses nothing by the new insights into the Ruth story. When all is told, he stands taller than ever as one of the strongest, most admirable male characters in all of Scripture.

Four Guiding Principles

I hope you are as eager as I am to launch into this story. But before we proceed, let me lay out four important principles that have shaped this study and which, I believe, are powerful tools that open up richer insights, no matter what portion of God's Word we happen to be studying.

First and foremost, God is the true hero of the story. No matter how captivating the other characters may be, our top priority is to discover what the Bible reveals about God. Often Ruth is viewed as a simple love story, a shining moment at a dark time in Israelite history. While Ruth teaches us a lot about love, the book is also packed with deep insights about God and his relationship with his people. This can be said about any portion of the Bible. So, whenever we study God's Word, our main quest is always to discover what he is telling us about himself. If we marginalize God or make someone else the focal point, we will *always* miss the main message of the book. Always.

Second, Eve's legacy—God's creation blueprint for women —is key to understanding Naomi and Ruth.[3] God created women to be his *image bearers*—to know him, to become like him, and to represent him in their interactions with others. As theologians, Naomi and Ruth understand that the world revolves around God. Their mission is to center themselves on him—to trust him and to advance his kingdom.

They do that as *ezer-warriors*,[4] fighting battles he places in their path. God has created women to be warriors, and he stations us on all sorts of battlefronts every day of our lives. On the surface, Ruth and Naomi's battles seem mundane and insignificant. Little do they know what their everyday struggles to survive will actually achieve.

Furthermore (and this is where Boaz comes in), the *Blessed Alliance*—God's design from creation that men and women join forces in serving him together—is alive and well in the book of Ruth.[5] Interactions between Boaz and the women are some of the most instructive aspects of the book. The three present us with an exquisite picture of how God intends for men and women to partner for his purposes—a powerful gospel model that today's church desperately needs to see.

Third, the Bible is an ancient book, written in a culture that is completely foreign to the world we know. In some ways, Naomi's world was even foreign to the original readers of Ruth, who were living after the time of King David. To close the gap, the narrator occasionally inserts explanations to bring these ancient readers up to speed. This means, of course, that the distance between Naomi's world and ours is even greater—enough to make us feel at points that we are living on a different planet. Surprising as this may sound, a Western, American, middle-class point of view can actually interfere with our understanding of God's Word.

The story of Naomi and Ruth takes place against the backdrop of an ancient patriarchal culture. If we want to grasp the message, we must enter Naomi's world. We can do this better with the help of our sisters in the Third World whose cultures more closely resemble the ancient biblical culture. The payoff is well worth the effort, especially in biblical passages that focus explicitly on women, as we are about to see. Against the ancient patriarchal backdrop, the Bible's strong message for women packs a punch that we completely miss when we ignore the cultural context.

Last, the author of this narrative did not break the story apart into chapters and verses. Artistically crafted, the whole book hangs together as a perfectly cohesive literary unit. The beginning, middle, and end are all deeply interrelated—seamlessly interconnected by plot, character development, and a rich undercurrent of themes. So, for example, we must be careful to carry Naomi's pain and Ruth's radical vow with us from chapter 1 to the barley field, the threshing floor, and the legal proceedings at the Bethlehem gate. Along the way, we will observe changes in Naomi, Ruth, and Boaz, for all three evolve and mature in their faith as the story progresses. We will also be tracking important themes that the author weaves through the story.

A SURPRISE BEGINNING

You can usually rely on a good storyteller to come up with a surprise ending. The author of the book of Ruth does not disappoint. The ending of the story is packed with unexpected outcomes to amaze any reader. Hopefully, by the time we finish, we will be filled with awe and gratitude over the transforming power of God's goodness in women's lives and gripped by a larger vision of what God will do through us today. What is unique about this little masterpiece, however, is the fact that the story also has a surprise beginning.

The opening verses introduce a man named Elimelech, his wife, Naomi, and their two sons, giving the impression that the story you are about to hear is about the men—Elimelech and his sons, Mahlon and Kilion. Yet, after introducing this trio of male characters, the story takes an unexpected twist that keeps the reader glued to the page.

In five short verses, death wipes the men off the scene, leaving three grieving widows behind. In a male-centered culture that ascribed value to women based on their relationships to men, these husbandless, sonless women hold no interest to anyone. In many minds, especially in the minds of the three women themselves, the story is over. Nothing is left to tell. Yet ironically, this is where the narrative heats up as the biblical spotlight settles on Naomi and an all-female cast. Now the real story begins.

And so we begin our journey by entering a downward spiral of suffering with Naomi, the female Job, who from ground zero of her own life wants to know, "Is God good for women?"

DISCUSSION QUESTIONS

1. Describe a time when you (or someone you love) questioned God's goodness to women.

2. Did you (or they) feel free or afraid to ask and wrestle with your question? Why or why not?

3. Why does the subject of God inevitably come up when we are going through difficult circumstances or experiencing great losses?

4. What potential harm might come from stifling our questions about God?

5. How does the description of Naomi as "a female Job"—an icon of suffering—seem to bring this question out into the open and invite us to ask our questions too?

6. Why is it surprising for the Bible to speak honestly and openly about God's people when they suffer and are going through

deep spiritual crises, instead of concealing these negative stories?

7. Why is this honesty important to you personally?

8. How do our questions draw us to God, instead of driving us away?

Chapter One

LOOKING AT GOD
FROM GROUND ZERO

"So much for your God."

Those scornful words were aimed at a friend of mine as she stood with coworkers around the office television watching the tragic events of September 11 unfold. The unexpected barb came from the business colleague next to her, a man with whom she had shared her faith on numerous occasions, all to no effect. His words—uttered as the second World Trade Center Tower collapsed—verbalized what a lot of horrified people (including my friend) were thinking.

In our post–9/11 world, we've watched Christian leaders confronted by journalists who want to know, "Where was God on September 11?" It's a fair question, whether we like it or not. Still, I always cringe when I hear it because I'm not sure how to answer the question. It doesn't cause me to doubt God's existence, but it does force me to admit there's a lot about God I don't understand. To simply say, "His ways are not our ways," doesn't ultimately satisfy or soothe a wounded heart. The consternation we all feel is the price we pay for life in a fallen world.

Yes, September 11 troubles me. But there are other troubling days on the calendar—not just the ones that make the evening news, but also the ones that end up in my journal. Thumbing through the pages of my private reflections, I come across entries written in the middle of sleepless nights, when anxiety took over and robbed me of rest. When my personal world is falling apart and something or someone precious is at stake, it is frightening when God doesn't show up to hold things together, especially when I'm begging him to come. No voice calls out from heaven to calm the troubled waters. There's no miraculous healing or change of heart. No unseen army of angels shields me from disaster. Instead of getting better, things are only getting worse. My mother used to tell me, "Things always look worse at night." For the most part, I believe her. But some of the troubles that keep me from sleeping look just as bad in the morning.

Christians are great pretenders. We tell ourselves it's not supposed to be this way for Christians, and so we resort to a cover-up. For the sake of the gospel, we don't want to let on (especially in front of a watching world) that things aren't working out so well. We try to smooth things over for God, send in our best damage-control team to deal with these embarrassing questions, and polish up God's reputation. We feel it's our Christian duty to look our best. We can't afford to show our flaws. Let's give the world (and each other) the airbrushed version of ourselves as proof that the Christian life really works.

God won't and doesn't participate in this kind of masquerade. If the Bible tells us anything, it is that this world is fraught with perils and hardships. Eugene Peterson is candid enough to tell us the truth: "No literature is more realistic and honest in facing the harsh facts of life than the Bible. At no time is there the faintest suggestion that the life of faith exempts us from difficulties.... On every page of the Bible there is recognition that faith encounters troubles."[1] We are broken ourselves and can't escape the brokenness and loss of our fallen world.

An honest reading of the Bible reveals a God who does not shy away from awkward questions. In fact, he almost seems to welcome them. The ruined lives of Job and Naomi pose disturbing questions about God without censorship—a surprising indication that the disconcerting questions journalists are asking about

God are not off-limits for us either. An honest reading also reveals a God who doesn't explain himself. He didn't tell Job about his earlier conversation with Satan and he didn't give Naomi three good reasons why her world fell apart. Both sufferers went to their graves with their whys unanswered and the ache of their losses still intact. But somehow, because they met God in their pain, both also gained a deeper kind of trust in him that weathers adversity and refuses to let go of God. Their stories coax us to get down to the business of wrestling with God instead of chasing rainbows and to employ the same kind of brutal honesty that they did, if we dare.

A FEMALE JOB

So what was Naomi thinking as she sifted through the ruins of her life and contemplated the God she had believed in since she was a child? Did she mutter a "So much for your God" to herself? What did her two Moabite daughters-in-law think after witnessing the tsunamis that swept away Naomi's world without a whisper of interference from her God? Not only were they eyewitnesses of their mother-in-law's losses, they were caught in the tidal wave of her sorrows and were drowning in grief themselves.

The collapse of Naomi's world did not happen in a day but was spread out over years of heartache and tragedy. There were no heroic rescue workers rushing in to carry her to safety, no grim-faced news anchors choking back the tears as they reported a relentless sequence of disasters that sent her into shock, no half-mast flags or weeping nation to grieve her losses. Naomi's grief was a long time coming, the buildup of years of major disappointments, setbacks, and losses retold by the biblical narrator as cold facts in five short verses, without so much as a sigh or a tear.

I never connected emotionally with Naomi's losses until I heard her compared to the legendary sufferer Job. That got my attention. Until then, her sufferings seemed to serve as props to set up the real drama—the love story between Ruth and Boaz. In my eagerness to get to the part where Boaz enters the narrative, I stepped over a shattered Naomi and, in the process, missed the real power of the story—a story of a woman's struggle with God.

Glossing over Naomi's agonies comes at a high price, for by minimizing Naomi's pain, we inadvertently minimize our own. We owe it to Naomi and to ourselves to stop and contemplate the collapsing towers in Naomi's life—to sit with her for a while at ground zero—for without a better grasp of her sufferings, we will miss the impact of her doubts about God and the power of the Gospel of Ruth.

ENTERING NAOMI'S WORLD

Naomi's sufferings didn't begin in Moab but started back in Bethlehem with a famine—a frightening humanitarian crisis that is difficult for prosperous, well-fed America to fathom. When the average American says, "I'm starving," it is a prelude to a midnight raid on a well-stocked refrigerator or a sudden trip to the nearest fast food restaurant. Sometimes we starve ourselves in a determined quest for fashionable thinness. It says a lot about us that we are able to pass over the word "famine" in the biblical text without at least pausing to shudder at the horrors this word implies. Prosperity puts us at a disadvantage when it comes to comprehending the devastating conditions that drove Naomi and her family from famine-ravaged Bethlehem—which means "house of bread"—to Moab (today's Jordan), where there was food.

A documentary report of a bone-weary Somali woman brought me closer to the true face of famine. Barefoot and hungry, she trudged for ten days over hot dusty roads to reach the UNICEF mother-and-child clinic in Waajid town. Back home, two of her six children lay in small shallow graves, victims of the famine still threatening the rest of her family. Moaning listlessly at her breast, her emaciated one-year-old was too weak to nurse and in desperate need of medical attention. When the ground hardens and cracks under blistering skies, parents will do anything—even move to Moab—to save their children's lives.

Naomi's famine came during a notoriously dark period in Israel's history—the days when the judges governed. The book of Judges is an appalling letdown after the glory days of Moses and Joshua, where we read to our dismay that the following generation "knew neither the LORD nor what he had done for Israel" (Judges 2:10). God raised up judges to rescue them from the trouble they brought on themselves and to lead them back to Yahweh. Biblical writers tell us the people habitually did "what was right in their own eyes" (17:6; 21:25, NRSV), which is just another way of saying they turned their backs on God. From there, it was a short step for the Israelites to start worshiping the idols of their neighbors and to embrace their pagan ways. A terrible downward spiral ensued.[2] Catastrophic judgments followed, taking the form of military invasions, government collapse, foreign oppressors, and *famines*.[3]

Just as the rains fall on the good and the evil, so God's judgments on an adulterous Israel fell on the faithful as well. Indications seem to place Naomi and her husband, Elimelech, in this latter group, which makes their suffering all the more pitiable. Famine drove Elimelech's family from their home. It must have been a bitter pill to swallow. I can only imagine Naomi's thoughts as she plodded along the dusty road to Moab with her husband, their two boys, and other famine refugees. "Promised Land? House of Bread? Chosen people? If God loves us so much, why doesn't he help us?" But famine was only the beginning of Naomi's troubles.

An Outsider in Moab

If you've ever lived in a foreign country and don't possess the chameleon's natural ability to blend into your surroundings, you will have some sympathy for what Naomi endured after the move to Moab. Immigrants aren't always welcome. Even in America's melting pot—where all but Native Americans descended from immigrants—we no longer greet new arrivals with open arms, but with raised eyebrows or something worse. Foreigners here and throughout the world face the inevitable difficulties of language barriers, cultural gaffs, bouts with homesickness and depression, and the sense that you're never really "one of them." After migrating from Judah, Naomi lived as an outsider among the Moabites. A long history of political tensions between Moab and Israel certainly didn't ease matters any.[4]

Although the relocation of Elimelech's family to ride out the famine in Moab was originally intended as a "sojourn," it gradually settled into a more permanent arrangement that lasted over ten years. Without the modern blessings of e-mail to keep in touch with family or of El Al Airlines to facilitate occasional visits from relatives or a quick trip home, Naomi's longings for home went unrelieved. Homesickness was minor, however, compared to what happened next.

A MOUNTING DEATH TOLL

The death of Naomi's husband was a milestone she never meant to cross. The loss of a spouse is hard enough to bear. But when the death occurs on foreign soil, the tragedy takes on new dimensions. I remember the shock my family felt when my Uncle George—halfway around the world on a trip of a lifetime with his wife and three children—telegraphed us that he had just buried his beloved wife in Pakistan. None of us ever envisioned their great adventure turning into a nightmare or his coming home to the States as a widower.

Elimelech's death hurled Naomi into grief that ebbed and flowed for the rest of her life. But for Naomi, as for other widows with children, there was little time to think of herself or to nurse her own grief because of the pressing needs of her two sons. The death of Elimelech catapulted her into the ranks of single parents—a daunting task in any era or culture. At least Naomi still had her sons.

Naomi's boys were the family future and their mother's glory. In a culture that measured a woman's value by the number of sons she produced, Naomi was a woman worthy of honor for giving birth to Mahlon and Kilion. Her accomplishments in childbirth meant the Elimelech family line was a sturdy double strand. Even the woes of widowhood were blunted somewhat for

Naomi by the fact that she had double insurance coverage for the future—two sons to carry on her husband's name and to care for her in her old age.

We aren't told the ages of Mahlon and Kilion when their father died. We only know they were young and as yet unmarried. This posed a serious problem in Moab, where finding suitable brides for young, marriageable Israelite males was next to impossible. I thought of Naomi when I heard a mother confiding to friends her disapproval of her son's fiancée, a Christian girl who didn't quite measure up to this mother's hopes for a daughter-in-law.

The problem for Naomi, however, wasn't that the girls her sons brought home were less than perfect. Ruth and Orpah weren't even in the running. As Moabites—pagan worshipers of Chemosh, a god that demanded child sacrifice—these women represented a believing Israelite mother's worst fears. The Moab nation descended from an incestuous encounter between Lot and his oldest daughter—distant relatives from the shady side of Abraham's family tree.[5] Mosaic Law banned Moabites from the assembly of Yahweh's people to the tenth generation.[6] Sordid chapters in Israel's past that resulted from romantic alliances with Moabite women[7] gave Naomi further cause for alarm.

From the perspective of the local culture, there were problems too. In the ancient culture, fathers typically negotiated arranged marriages, usually with an eye toward forging advantageous relationships with other families. The narrator omits the details, but we already know that in addition to the drawbacks of their immigrant Israelite status and the absence of a father, Naomi and her sons were without land, wealth, or other assets that might attract a Moabite family's interest. Fathers in Moab's high society would not be inclined to marry off their daughters to the likes of Mahlon and Kilion. It is difficult to argue that the brides Naomi's sons took for themselves were the cream of the crop of young Moabite women.

Things went from bad to worse. A decade passed, and neither Orpah nor Ruth conceived. Calculating from a woman's normal monthly cycle, Naomi and her daughters-in-law suffered as many as 240 separate and increasingly devastating disappointments in a culture where it was a woman's business to produce children. In addition to the heartache this double barrenness brought to the women personally, their inability to conceive was a catastrophe for the family, for the survival of Elimelech's line depended on the birth of at least one male to carry on the family name, and in the ancient world survival was everything.

During those agonizing years, how many sleepless nights did Naomi suffer—nights of tears and pleadings, begging God to step in and stop the madness? Where was he? Why didn't he do something? The future of her family hung in the balance, and God didn't seem to be listening. Yet, despite the beleaguered Naomi's prayers, trouble marched forward like an unopposed army trampling underfoot what was left of her life, every last cherished hope and dream. Naomi shared the psalmist's exasperation. "Why, O LORD, do you stand far off? Why do you hide yourself in times of trouble?" (Psalm 10:1).

Ten lean years of double infertility finally ended, not with a positive pregnancy test, but with the unthinkable—the premature deaths of *both* of Naomi's sons. This was the worst possible scenario for a widow. The light had gone out in the Elimelech household—extinguished on Naomi's watch. Annihilation was a fate the ancients feared most. The deaths of Mahlon and Kilion bereaved Naomi of her beloved children, wiped out her life's work as a woman, and brought the curtain down with a merciless thud on the future. When they buried Naomi's sons, they were essentially burying Naomi too.

Overnight, her already diminished social status hit rock bottom, and Naomi was suddenly at risk. Without a male connection, she had no place in society and no source of income. Without a male protector, she was fair game for the unscrupulous who regularly preyed on helpless widows. Alone in a male-dominated world, Naomi was cast upon the mercy of a society that had little interest in her. But Naomi's social standing wasn't the only thing that was going down.

The Dark Night of the Soul

Christians in adversity sometimes relate glowing stories of an overwhelming sense of God's presence, a nearness, an unexpected surge of strength, a comfort that came just when they felt they couldn't go on. But for Naomi there was no spiritual renewal, no rejuvenation of her inner strength. Instead of finding comfort in God, she, like her counterpart Job, found that thinking about God only made things worse.

We'd like to think Naomi's faith is rugged enough to endure the blows of famine, displacement, widowhood, childlessness, and marginalization without flinching—that she stands firm, maintains a vibrant faith, and praises God in the darkness. But she is battered by affliction, and her heated outbursts against God shock our spiritual sensibilities. She is not unlike the shell-shocked Elie Wiesel, who emerged from the holocaust still convinced of God's existence, but having lost all hope in God's goodness. "Never shall I forget those moments which murdered my God and my soul and turned my dreams to dust. Never shall I forget these things, even if I am condemned to live as long as God Himself. Never."[8] The decimated Naomi retains her faith in God—and even some measure of hope that he will bless her daughters-in-law. But she no longer looks for him to bless her and lays the blame for her misery at Yahweh's feet. He has become her enemy. He has raised his hand against her, emptying her of everything she ever held dear.

Somehow we've convinced ourselves that the more mature we become as Christians—and both Naomi and Job were seasoned believers—the thicker our spiritual skin will become. We'll be resilient in adversity. It's a sign of spiritual failure (so we tell ourselves) when suffering gets the better of us and our faith in God gets shaky. Such notions (which aren't supported by Scripture, certainly not by the legacies of Naomi and Job) get in the way of our spiritual growth and block us from engaging the God who pursues us in our pain. To tell the truth, when the full force of our sufferings hits us, no matter how long we've walked with God or how much theology we've mastered, faith in God can take an awful beating.

The narrator does not intend for readers to watch as distant spectators while the anguished Naomi blurts out her true feelings toward God, but to enter the story as this female Job speaks out for us. Her story and Job's are in our Bibles so we will learn to be honest as they were about how badly we are hurting, to go ahead and ask the questions that are smoldering inside. Naomi's story invites us to admit we've been flattened too, that we don't understand what's happening to us, and that, even after walking with God for years, we still struggle to trust him. By spotlighting Naomi's ordeal, the narrator gives us permission to voice the thoughts and questions we are fighting so desperately to suppress. And in some mysterious way we meet God in our desperation.

For the moment, Naomi holds her tongue. The time will come when she speaks openly of matters of the soul, although not in lengthy polemical speeches as we hear from Job and his three friends. Naomi's words are few, though her pain was every bit as deep and her losses as devastating. Some may see this as an overstatement, but I think Naomi actually out-Jobed Job. Both tragically lose their families and the life they worked to build. But Job is not alone. He still has his wife and a community to surround him (such as they are). Job is not an immigrant and he is not a woman.

God will answer Naomi too, not through a voice speaking out of the storm as he spoke to Job, but in the simple touch of a human embrace as Naomi halts on the long, hopeless road back to Bethlehem.

"X" MARKS THE SPOT

Embedded in the middle of Oxford's bustling Broad Street is a simple stone cross. Every year thousands of foreign tourists gazing up at the spires of Oxford's skyline and local pedestrians preoccupied with everyday errands walk over this historic marker without realizing they are treading on sacred ground. The unpretentious "X" marks the spot where in 1555 Anglican Bishops Nicholas Ridley and Hugh Latimer were burned at the stake for their Christian beliefs and entered eternity in a blaze of courage and glory. "Be of good comfort, Master Ridley, and play the man!" the dying Latimer cried out. "We shall this day light such a candle by God's grace in England, as I trust shall never be put out." It was a moment of such significance in English history that Oxford does not want to forget.

If I had my way, there would be a large stone "X" embedded in the middle of the road that runs between Moab and Bethlehem to mark the spot where Naomi stops to send her daughters-in-law back to Moab. This is one moment in biblical history that has never been given the earthshaking significance it deserves. I'm embarrassed to admit how many times I have walked over this very spot in my Bible without realizing I was treading on holy ground.

What causes this scene literally to rock the entire book and ranks it among the most dramatic moments in all of biblical history is not (as we have supposed) the tender display of Ruth's deep devotion to her mother-in-law, but the collision that takes place between the weight of evidence Naomi has mounted against God and the radical choice Ruth makes. Naomi's decision to emancipate her daughters-in-law—the first rule-breaking event in the book—precipitates a crisis that forces both daughters-in-law to make what on the surface appears to be a pragmatic decision, but which, when examined more closely, reveals that matters of the greatest import are afoot. The choices made on this historic spot will not only shape the very souls of all three women, they will alter the course of Israel's history and advance the redemptive purposes of God. As I said, there ought to be a permanent marker on this road to keep the world from forgetting what has happened here.

A Case for Moab

Naomi goes against cultural conventions and her own self-interest when she relinquishes two able-bodied young women who are duty-bound[9] to her by marriage and whose departure will reduce her family to one. Given the circumstances, it is the only compassionate thing to do. Naomi is a realist. She cherishes no illusion that Bethlehem means a fresh start for her or for them. Naomi is postmenopausal. Her childbearing years have expired. She has no value as a wife. As potential brides, her daughters-in-law have two strikes against them: a long history of barrenness and their Moabite identity. In Bethlehem they lack the necessary father figure to negotiate a marriage for them. Naomi cannot bring herself to drag them along with her into such a hopeless future. Their best chance for security is in returning to their roots.

Some speculate that Naomi has intended all along to send her daughters-in-law back to Moab,[10] but waits until they have gone far enough from Moab to prevent them from talking her out of leaving. What is *not* a matter of speculation is Naomi's ironclad determination to resume the journey to Bethlehem without them. Her words do not contain a drop of false pretense. She is not urging them to return to Moab—testing their loyalty—when she really longs for them to stay with her. She means for them to go and formally releases both women from any legal, moral, or familial responsibility to her. She argues, coerces, implores, and all but hires a cab to take them back. Did she ever imagine her task would be so hard?

Naomi begins by simply instructing Orpah and Ruth to go back to Moab, adding her prayer that Yahweh will reward their kindness to her and to her sons by blessing them with rest in the homes of new husbands. Her words are met with astonishing resistance. The countryside is filled with sobs as the trio weeps inconsolably and the two young widows cling to Naomi. Clearly, Naomi has underestimated the bonds of grief and love.

Undeterred, Naomi tries again, this time spelling out in no uncertain terms the bitter fact that there is no future in Bethlehem. Even the normal provisions for young widows do not apply here, for Naomi has no surviving sons to marry the widows of Mahlon and Kilion. Bethlehem can only promise permanent widowhood for all three. Moab offers hope.

Ironically, Naomi's words seem to have their greatest effect on her. It is as if by verbalizing the awful truth about the death of her own hopes that the painful reality of her losses sinks in with renewed force. It is a Job moment, when she can no longer stifle what her sufferings imply about God. The dam that for so long has been holding back a tidal wave of anger and despair bursts open in a flood of bitter hopelessness. "No, my daughters. It is more bitter for me than for you, because the LORD's hand has gone out against me!" (Ruth 1:13). Her words echo Job's, who in a similar mode complained, "He has made me his target; his archers surround me … the Almighty, who has made me taste bitterness of soul" (Job 16:12 – 13; 27:2).[11]

Her arguments hit their mark with Orpah. She has seen and heard enough. Clearly all signs point to Moab, and she will take her freedom and go home. After the three weep again, Orpah dries her eyes, says her good-byes, and turns back, leaving Naomi and her clinging sister-in-law behind.

Before we finish with Orpah, it is important to note that she serves an important role in the story. The narrator intends for us to contrast her with Ruth, not because Orpah is selfish or wicked, but because she is sensible. Naomi has praised her character, and Orpah has just exhibited deep devotion to Naomi by refusing her first opportunity to go home. Here, however, she displays good common sense and does what anyone reading the story for the first time expects her to do. She weighs the facts and submits to her mother-in-law's counsel. She is only following the logical trajectory of the evidence and doing what she has been told. She heads back to Moab with Naomi's full approval. At the same time her actions create a striking contrast with the truly radical nature of Ruth's choice.

WHEN NAOMI AND RUTH COLLIDE

After Orpah's departure an emotionally depleted Naomi gathers strength to deal with her remaining daughter-in-law. Orpah's choice gives Naomi a new argument—a touch of peer pressure—that she levels at Ruth. Pointing down the road, she argues, "Look … your sister-in-law is going back to her people and her gods. Go back with her" (Ruth 1:15).

When Naomi guides Ruth's gaze to the disappearing form of her sister-in-law and describes Orpah's actions in *theological* terms—a going back to her people *and* to her gods—something takes hold of Ruth that is bigger than both of them. It is as though, in an instant, the floodlights go on in the darkened stadium of Ruth's soul, bringing the issues into razor-sharp focus. Despite Naomi's urgings, at its core, this choice is not about geography, family loyalty, or the future. This decision is about God.

With startling determination, Ruth embraces Naomi, resolutely digs in her heels, and insists that the arguments stop. "Do not pressure me to desert you, to give up following you" (Ruth 1:16, Hubbard translation).[12] This is no halfhearted decision, but a commitment to the grave. "Where you go I will go, and where you stay I will stay. Your people will be my people and your God my God. Where you die I will die, and there I will be buried" (Ruth 1:16–17).

To squelch any further debate on the subject, Ruth goes over Naomi's head by appealing to Naomi's God—the God Naomi has just identified as the enemy—to judge her severely if she fails to keep her word. "*Thus* may Yahweh do to me and more so if even death itself separates me from you" (Ruth 1:17, Hubbard translation, emphasis added). Ruth accompanies this vow with a violent gesture—perhaps a slashing motion towards her own throat—as if to say, "May God do 'thus' to me if I break my vow to you."[13]

The impact on Naomi is impossible to imagine. Could there be a stronger collision of words than Naomi's despairing, "The LORD's hand has gone out against me," and Ruth's resolutely opposite, "Your God will be my God"? What kind of logic is this?

The explanation we usually settle on is that Ruth is so devoted and close to her mother-in-law that she simply cannot bear to leave her. Without a doubt, Ruth's loyal love for Naomi is one of the strongest themes flowing through this story—a love that in the end will prove more extraordinary and selfless than anyone could guess. But it is difficult to argue from this text for a chummy relationship between the two women. Interaction between Naomi and Ruth following this exchange doesn't even hint of closeness between them. Instead, Naomi withdraws in stony silence: "When Naomi saw that she was firmly determined to go on with her, she said nothing more to her" (Ruth 1:18, Hubbard translation).

When they finally arrive in Bethlehem, Naomi laments (with Ruth standing right beside her), "I went away full, but the LORD has brought me back empty" (Ruth 1:21). "Empty" is hardly what you'd expect to hear from a relieved mother-in-law safely back from the brink of nearly losing her precious Ruth.

In silence, a bewildered Naomi collects her possessions and resumes the journey to Bethlehem with her unbending daughter-in-law at her side. This is the first time Ruth breaks the rules. It will not be the last. What possesses her to make such a choice? Why does she deliberately sabotage her own future?

THE SOUL OF A WOMAN

By his own account C. S. Lewis (who in 1926 was suspended somewhere between atheism and the gospel) identified a bus ride home up Headington Hill from Magdalen College in Oxford as the moment "God closed in on me."

> I became aware that I was holding something at bay, or shutting something out. Or, if you like, that I was wearing some stiff clothing, like corsets, or even a suit of armor, as if I were a lobster. I felt myself being, there and then, given a free choice. I could open the door or keep it shut; I could unbuckle the armor or keep it on.... The choice appeared to be momentous but it was also strangely unemotional. I was moved by no desires or fears. In a sense I was not moved by anything. I chose to open, to unbuckle, to loosen the rein. I say, "I chose," yet it did not really seem possible to do the opposite.... You could argue that I was not a free agent, but I am more inclined to think this came nearer to being a perfectly free act than most that I have ever done.[14]

By the time the bus reached the top of the hill, a sinner had crossed over into safety.

The moment may not have been as unemotional for the young Moabitess as it was for Lewis, but somewhere along the road to Bethlehem God closed in on Ruth. To the casual observer, Ruth was simply embracing Naomi. But Ruth was also embracing Naomi's God. Scholars point out that this is the spot where Ruth the Moabitess chose to become an Israelite—a true follower of Yahweh—a conversion of faith expressed in a vow of radical self-sacrifice to Naomi. Although Ruth's actions clearly went against the grain of conventional wisdom and even her own natural instincts of self-interest, no doubt Ruth would concur with Lewis in saying, "It did not really seem possible to do the opposite."

We can only guess what other factors may have contributed to this turning point in Ruth's life.[15] Coming from the darkness of a pagan culture, she surely saw the differences when she entered a family of believing Israelites, heard their history, watched them interact with one another and with their neighbors, and observed them in the aftermath of three tragic deaths. They weren't perfect, to be sure. But when you're living in darkness, as Ruth was, even a little light can make a powerful difference.

Ruth may not have wrestled through the philosophical issues as rigorously as C. S. Lewis did. She did not see a vision of blazing light like the one on the road to Damascus that turned Saul of Tarsus around or a burning bush like the one that caught Moses' attention. But she was as thoroughly reoriented as these men were, and she would impact her world as profoundly as they did theirs. To borrow from New Testament language, Ruth discovered in Yahweh "the pearl of greatest price," and she leaves everything behind to follow him. She might lose the world, but she has saved her soul. The road to Bethlehem marks a stupendous moment—the miraculous redirecting of a human heart that only God can cause. For her part, the young Moabitess never looks back.

THE GOSPEL OF RUTH

If scholars compare Naomi to Job, they compare Ruth the Moabitess to Abraham. The faith Ruth exhibits here rivals what the wealthy patriarch Abraham did in leaving his homeland and family for an unknown land. But Ruth leaves on her own, empty-handed, against intense pressure to the contrary from Naomi and her own woman's heart. Ahead of her lies poverty and an uphill struggle to survive. Instead of pursuing the slim prospects she has for a husband and security in Moab, she devotes herself for life to an old woman and sets her face toward the unknown Bethlehem.

Unlike Abraham, Ruth's decision is unbolstered by God's promises of great blessing along the way or any visible props from her circumstances that might reinforce her choice. If anything, Ruth's future is grimmer than Naomi's, for now Ruth will be the foreigner and, because she is young, she faces a longer stretch of adversity ahead than her aging mother-in-law. But with both eyes open to the consequences of her actions, Ruth slams and bolts the door on her own future. She clings tenaciously to the despairing Naomi, then cries out for the heavens to fall on her if she fails to keep her word. It takes my breath away.

Whenever I tell the story of Ruth, I often hear women say, "I want to be a Ruth." I hear that refrain even more often, the deeper I take them into her story. Ruth stands out among all of the biblical narratives as a powerful example of a person whose faith in God emboldens her with stunning courage. She gives us one of the strongest examples in all of Scripture of faith in action and, as future scenes will show, a risk-it-all determination to live as a child of God. She is a true *ezer*. I want to be a Ruth too.

But we also need to take a long hard look at Naomi, for if the truth were known, there's a bit of Naomi in all of us. Hopefully, we won't come near her Job-like level of suffering, but we live in a fallen world and all of us, sooner or later, will drink deeply from its sorrows. Naomi is here to remind us that—in those long, bewildering phases of God's silence—our struggles are real and we can be honest about the state of our hearts. Her full story reminds us that our struggles are also important and that, even when there's nothing left but rubble, God is mysteriously at work in the mess.

This is the Gospel of Ruth—a shaft of light across the empty blackness of a broken life—a woman's radical faith that refuses to say, "So much for your God." Ruth's brand of faith is not some free-floating optimism or a Cinderella belief in a "happily-ever-after" that awaits. Both Ruth and Naomi will grieve to their graves over loved ones they buried in Moab. Ruth's faith is grounded in the God who created her and who reveals himself in creation, in history, and in his people. Centuries down the road, in the very town where Ruth and Naomi are heading, he will reveal himself fully in Jesus.

Ruth is a powerful reminder that the most important thing in all of life—the purpose for which we were all created—is to know the God who made us and to walk through life as his child, no matter what it costs us. Even when we are standing at ground zero—when we are hurting, God is silent, and our suffering makes no sense—we have no other place to go. And so Ruth clings to Naomi and turns her face toward Bethlehem.

Although, for the moment, this message of hope doesn't penetrate Naomi's heart, God will get through to her in time. But before we move on to see what happens next, we have some important groundwork to do.

Ruth and Naomi embody two figures sighted frequently on the biblical landscape: the *widow* and the *barren woman*. Widowhood and barrenness account for some of the greatest sufferings of the women of the Bible. A deeper understanding of both is crucial to unlocking the meaning of the book of Ruth. What we seem to overlook, however, is the fact that widowhood and barrenness are more than plot elements. They are rich and powerful theological themes that run through Scripture and which, when unearthed, reveal God's amazing heart for women and the power of what he is doing in our lives today. In the following two chapters, the widow and the childless woman become our teachers, bringing us a vital message that the church has often overlooked.

DISCUSSION QUESTIONS

1. What caused Naomi to be angry with God?

2. What did Naomi believe about God?

3. Describe a situation in your life where you shared Naomi's view of God.

4. How do our circumstances influence our beliefs about God?

5. Why are our questions about God so important?

6. Why did Ruth reject Naomi's counsel?

7. How do our beliefs about God influence how we see our struggles?

8. What does Ruth teach us about God?

Chapter Two

LEFT BEHIND —
A WOMAN ON HER OWN

Nine out of ten wives will spend some portion of their lives in widowhood.

The first time I came across that statistic in an article I was reading, a shudder shot straight down my spine. Ninety percent! Whenever I think about that statistic (and I try hard not to), I feel an overwhelming urge to stop what I'm doing and dash into the next room or phone the seminary to make sure Frank is okay. I can't imagine living life without him. But who am I to think I'll end up in the lucky 10 percent?

The American Cancer Society informs us one in eight women is diagnosed with breast cancer every year. That puts us all on red alert. We go religiously for annual mammograms. We join campaigns to raise money for breast cancer research. Our calendars are flagged so we won't forget our monthly self-exam. If the odds of getting breast cancer rose to 50 percent, we'd be in an all-out panic. Yet we live in complete denial of a statistic that will devastate 90 percent of us — a loss that will leave many of us thinking our own lives have ended too. For some, it will happen more than once.

"Widow" is a label that has a way of suddenly affixing itself to a woman without her permission, often without warning, and certainly without apology for the drastic alterations it will bring into her life. Sometimes it comes upon a woman by stealth while she is sleeping or going about a normal day's business. Sometimes a husband literally simply slips through her fingers as she strokes his unresponsive hand and keeps anxious vigil by his hospital bedside. Sometimes, through the medium of modern technology, women watch their widowhood arrive live on CNN as a major catastrophe unfolds or some public figure is cut down.

Given the odds, it seems strange that whenever the subject of widows comes up, we usually think of our grandmother or some elderly aunt. We never think of ourselves. If you haven't pictured yourself in the numbers yet, consider these unhappy statistics.[1] Seventy-five percent of women are single when they die. One out of two married women who reaches the age of sixty-five will outlive her husband by fifteen years. Eighty to ninety percent of women will be responsible for the household income at some point in their adult lives. According to U.S. Census 2000 figures, there are nearly twelve million widows in this country alone. Notions of husbands protecting and providing for us go up in smoke when we study the data. Instead, we get the distinct impression that a lot of women are doing life alone, and their ranks are growing. The statistics do not even begin to measure the pain.

A Grief Observed

An older friend of mine recalled marveling as she watched television coverage of a blood-spattered, then black-veiled Jacqueline Kennedy making her way somberly, even regally, through the public events and ceremonies that followed President Kennedy's assassination in 1963. "Where did the First Lady find such composure and courage?" she wondered. Her question was answered years later when her own husband died, and she found herself moving numbly through funeral arrangements, coffin selection, and the gathering of friends. It was all so surreal—an out-of-body experience—a stage performance where she, as leading actress, couldn't begin to summon the emotions that truly fit the occasion. Only in private afterward, when everyone else had gone home, did the numbness wear off, exposing her to that first debilitating wave of grief. That was not the last time she came unglued.

I picked up a book about four young 9/11 widows.[2] Four times I journeyed down the path that led each woman to the man of her dreams. Four times I relived with them the horrors of the terrorist attack and watched their lives collapse with the Twin Towers. As I read, I lost track of the times my eyes blurred over. In the aftermath, they hit days when they couldn't get out of bed. They watched hours of mindless television during the day and took pills so they could sleep at night. Bound together by grief, these four women drew strength, solace, and the courage to live again from their friendships.

Friendship didn't offer Job much consolation when his world collapsed around him. He thought God was his friend, but his losses cast a shadow over God's goodness and justice. How could years of faithfulness to God add up to this? His closest friends suspected Job was hiding a scandal. Surely he deserved God's punishment for something he'd done wrong—some secret sin he had locked away in his closet to preserve his untarnished image.

Naomi's ruin stirred up the same deep struggle with God.[3] Her story and Job's suspend us between the painful realities of our fallen world and the God who calls us to trust him even when we're missing big pieces to the puzzle and he isn't giving answers. But similarities between Job and Naomi end as she heads down a dark and treacherous road that even Job is spared from traveling.

Bare Naked Ladies

Naomi and Job share a fundamental equality in that they have both lost everything. Their lives are in ruins, and their souls are drowning in grief. But the biggest distinction between them is the most obvious one—Naomi is a woman and Job is not. In the ancient patriarchal culture, his maleness counted for a lot. Doors might open to him, doors that are bolted shut to Naomi. Poverty is not inevitable for Job. He can work; he can rebuild. He may endure the unjust accusations of trusted friends, but he will not face degradation, discrimination, or physical abuse because he is male. He still retains a level of stature in the community, even though his character is under the microscope. If anyone raises a hand against him, Job has his rights and can take legal action. The offender will be prosecuted.

But the roof has caved in on Naomi. She faces a whole new layer of adversity because she is a woman in a culture that defers to men. Death strips her down until she stands nakedly before God without the usual props a woman counts on to justify her significance. This is where Naomi's story enlarges to encompass every woman who is (or fears ending up) alone regardless of the reason. Naomi's culture expected a woman to secure her place in society through marriage and motherhood. Although women today have more options, that expectation remains alive and well in the present, both in our culture and inside of us. The destruction of Naomi's wife and mother credentials sounds the death knell for her. Bereft, she floats on her own, disconnected from everything that gives her life meaning.

Widowhood precipitates Naomi's abrupt reentry into the world that solitary women have always inhabited. Life insurance and a sizeable bank account may cushion a woman's landing. But for everyone, the transition will be turbulent as she learns to manage life alone, often at a reduced standard of living and at a lower social status. Without a husband, she is half of a conversation. A fragment. The Ying without the Yang. In a world of couples, a widow feels like a leftover. But the messages that inform her of her diminished place in the world don't just come from inside. The outside world is sending signals that the world stops turning for the woman traveling through life alone.

One woman discovered that the loss of her husband brought an end to her social life. "Old friends gradually stopped including me when they got together," she observed. "I think it made them uncomfortable to have an odd number in the group."

That "leftover" feeling came over a widow when she walked into church without her husband for the first time and felt suddenly invisible. While her husband was still alive, people clustered around them for conversation after the worship service. Church leaders were courting her successful businessman husband for a leadership slot in the church. Now that she came by herself, she could slip in and out of church and hardly anyone noticed. "No one finds me interesting anymore without my husband."

Naomi shares that sentiment too. Minus the three men who gave her reasons to be part of the story, Naomi's words say it all: "I am empty" (see Ruth 1:21). Once brimming with life and dreams for the future, she is drained of hope and meaning. Her losses assault her value as a human being, her dignity as a child of God, her purpose in life. The culture will discard her; she believes God will too. In her nakedness, Naomi embodies an issue that concerns every human being—female or male. Hiding behind our marriages, families, careers, or bank accounts does not change the fact that underneath we are naked too. What happens to me if I lose my props? Who am I when there's nothing left but me? God's answer for Naomi covers the rest of us as well.

"Can This Be Naomi?"

If, instead of returning home, Naomi had been attending a class reunion a decade or two after graduation, not one former classmate would exclaim, "Naomi, you haven't changed a bit!" No makeup artist could conceal the dark circles, deep creases, and ashen coloring that etched defeat into her face. The returning Naomi's appearance is so altered that the sight of her throws the women of the village into a state of confusion. Job's three male friends reacted similarly. "When they saw him from a distance, they could hardly recognize him; they began to weep aloud, and they tore their robes and sprinkled dust on their heads.... No one said a word to him, because they saw how great his suffering was" (Job 2:12–13).

The women of Bethlehem thought this new arrival resembled their old neighbor Naomi, but they couldn't be sure.[4] In her commentary on Ruth, scholar Katharine Doob Sakenfeld explains, "The ten or more intervening years of toil and tragedy, let alone the hardships of the journey, have taken their toll on Naomi's appearance, and the expected clues for confirmation of identity that anyone looks to on sighting a long-lost friend are missing—no husband, no sons, only an accompanying woman stranger."[5]

Not only was Naomi unrecognizable to her old friends, she didn't recognize herself. It was hard to connect the satisfied wife and mother who departed Bethlehem over a decade ago in search of a better life with the useless, hollow shell of a widow who reentered the village today.

Naomi was in no mood for small talk with old neighbors. At the moment, the sore point was her name, which according to Hebrew custom was more than a label. It *defined* her. "Pleasant" or "lovely" were hardly the words that came to mind when anyone saw Elimelech's widow. Devastated by grief and with good reason to dread the future, the demoralized Naomi shed her old name for one that fit her better. " 'Don't call me Naomi [pleasant],' she told them. 'Call me Mara [bitter], because the Almighty has made my life very bitter. I went away full, but the LORD has brought me back empty' " (Ruth 1:20–21).

WOMEN IN THE SPOTLIGHT

Whenever the Bible highlights a woman, or when female themes like widowhood or barrenness bubble to the surface as they do in the book of Ruth, something extraordinary is happening. Generally speaking, men command the spotlight. Male stories are being told. Often, the only reason a woman gets written up is when she enters the story on the arm of a man. Male connections are a woman's entrée.

Miriam's claim to fame comes from being Moses' sister. People forget she was a prophetess and a leader of God's people in her own right.[6] Sarah and Hagar both rode on Abraham's coattails. Rebekah had her three minutes of fame because Abraham's son Isaac needed a wife and she matched the search criteria. In a patriarchal culture, everyone expected men to dominate the story. But even going back *before* human culture existed, the first woman arrived on the scene because it was "not good for the man to be alone."

The book of Ruth breaks all the rules, as two unescorted women take command of the storyline and men recede into the background. Naomi and Ruth do not climb to this high point in the action on the backs of men. They get here on their own. The three male names from the opening scenes are forgotten in the credits. They aren't the main point; Naomi and Ruth are. The men, if you can believe this, are actually marginal to the central plot. Even Boaz enters the story because of his connection to Naomi. "Now Naomi had a relative … whose name was Boaz" (Ruth 2:1).

This abrupt detour into the world of women is not the same thing as a television commercial suddenly catering to female viewers in the middle of an NFL football game to make sure the women don't lose interest. Biblical writers aren't tossing a bone to women so they'll "feel included." Nor are they tucking a Hallmark card into the combative, aggressive, adventuresome world of men—a gentle feminine touch to soften the rugged male landscape of the Old Testament. Matters of the gravest import for women and for men are taking place here. Besides, even with a female focus, the plot contains danger and the same heart-stopping suspense and courageous valor that readers expect to find in manly stories.

Contrary to what some might suspect, this severing of women's ties to men is not some defiant statement against men either—one more skirmish in the battle of the sexes. For Naomi and Ruth, the tragic turn of events in their lives is a bitter catastrophe, not a sign of progress. But the questions posed by the isolation of these widows need to be discussed under the most revealing light, for they challenge the thinking that a woman derives her value and significance from men or that anything can happen to us that will disqualify us from actively participating in God's mission for our world.

It may come as a shock to many readers that the popular view of Ruth as a romance is problematic too, but as we get deeper into the text, I suspect even diehard romantics will see we've lost a lot through this distortion. The love story approach operates under the assumption that what lands a woman on her feet (makes her life complete and fulfilling) is a man … and a baby. It leaves the mistaken impression that to jump-start the lives of Ruth and Naomi, the younger widow needs to get married and bear a child. Naomi coasts vicariously on the good things that happen to Ruth and just needs shelter and provisions, so she'll be comfortable for the duration of her life. We don't think of either woman in terms of mission, nor do we imagine that God is raising both women up for vital kingdom purposes. We do not notice how their story upends the culture's view of women or pause to weigh the big things God is doing through their actions.

To unpack the Bible's high view of women and the gospel-richness of their relationships with each other and with men, we need to study the untouched portrait of the Old Testament widow.

THE OLD TESTAMENT WIDOW

The Hebrew word for widow (*almanah*) cemented a widow's low rank in the ancient patriarchal culture. It comes from the root word *alem*, which means "unable to speak." In ancient patriarchal society, the widow was the "silent one"[7]—a definition that exposes a frightening vulnerability and a nightmarish powerlessness. Without a father, husband, son, or other male relative to speak and act in her defense, a woman had no voice, no legal rights, and no recourse against injustice.

Widowhood threw Naomi in with the weakest members of society—the widows, orphans, and foreigners. These at-risk individuals were defenseless because they lacked the necessary male connections to ensure their safety. In a world where the strong have historically (viciously at times) preyed on the weak, the dangers Naomi faced were not imaginary, but a brutal reality that Jesus exposed when he denounced the religious leaders of his day for "devouring widow's houses" (Mark 12:38–40; Luke 20:45–47). Evidently, trouble could come to her from any segment of society—ruffians as well as the refined, pagans as well as the pious.

Unlike widows in our culture today, ancient widows dressed the part, moving through the community as living symbols of sorrow and death. We all recall how Scarlet O'Hara of *Gone with the Wind* fame bristled at the drab black dresses society obliged her to wear during the prescribed time of mourning after her first husband died. It was a loss Scarlet never truly felt. So when the opportunity presented itself, she scorned propriety by dancing a jig in black with the notorious Captain Rhett Butler. Naomi never sensed the urge to dance. Her drab widow's garb coordinated perfectly with her inner state.

Her attire also marked her out as a target and trumpeted her vulnerability. But we don't need imaginary walks through the streets of ancient Bethlehem to get a sampling of what Naomi faced. Fresh and appalling examples abound in our world today.

City of Widows

Vrindavan, one of the Hindus' holiest places in India, is also known as the "City of Widows." Today, on the streets of Vrindavan, widows numbering in the thousands are everywhere. "Bent backed and white saried with shaven heads and outstretched begging bowls," discarded by their families, living like ascetics in abject poverty, sleeping on the ground, rising to fast and pray for a departed spouse, chanting for hours to earn a bowl of rice.[8]

One woman, widowed at seventeen, had been chanting for forty years and counting. "Encumbrances" to their families, many of these women have simply been thrown out of their homes or compelled to flee vindictive sons and daughters-in-law. They are often victims of physical and sexual abuse. Their sadness is palpable. "When we were young we never imagined this would be our end. I'm full of shame when I beg, thinking I am from a good family. It is the same with all the widows. Our usefulness is past. We are all rejects."[9]

In India, a woman loses all status the minute her husband dies—a fact appallingly confirmed in the past by *sati*, a rite where a widow was expected (or allowed) to throw herself on her husband's flaming funeral pyre. More than a diabolical practice, this "suicidal" act was also a graphic statement about the widow herself. According to *sati*, a woman's life was disposable after her husband was gone. *Sati* is illegal now in India, but one of Vrinda-van's widows muttered, "Sometimes I think even *sati* would have been preferable to the life of a widow."[10]

Naomi was not in danger of being burned alive when Elim-elech died, but in a culture that swept widows aside, she still faced plenty of danger. Words spoken by an Indian widow could have come from Naomi's lips. "This is not life. We all died the day our husbands died. How can anyone describe our pain? Our hearts are all on fire with sorrow. Now we just wait for the day when all this will end."[11]

The widows of Vrindavan make sense of Naomi's bitter lament. They also shed new light on Jesus' encounter with the widow from Nain who was burying her only son. As biblical scholar Bonnie Bowman Thurston notes in her insightful study on widows, "When Jesus raises this man from the dead, he is in fact restoring two persons to life in the community: the man and his mother."[12]

HEAVEN RULES

Juxtaposed against this abysmal background, God's view of women clashes at every point with how the world regards us, even with how we see ourselves. The widow becomes God's Exhibit A to teach the world (and his people in particular) how far we have to go before our thoughts and actions line up with his. This is not a lesson in civility or tips for being nicer to widows. That goal—while certainly an improvement over what widows often experience—is far too timid for God. He isn't interested in tin-kering with the existing system of human values so we can say we're doing things "better" than others. The gospel completely overhauls the human soul and introduces us to a radically new dimension of human relationships. God's view of the widow is light-years away from what we see when we look at her.

When widowhood or anything else alters a woman's life, the center of her identity doesn't disintegrate, for she is not defined or redefined by circumstances, relationships, her resume, or public opinion. God defines her. If you looked up "woman" in God's dictionary, you'd find the definition he set down as he drew up plans for the very first woman. He defined the woman as follows: "Image bearer; created in God's image and likeness; called to be fruitful and multiply, to rule and subdue." It's the same kingdom definition that he gave to the man. God issued definitions for the woman and the man when both were naked and their resumes were blank. Reduce them to their most elemental selves, and they are still God's image bearers. It ascribes to them the highest value imaginable.

God does not have a separate definition for widows or a footnote outlining an image bearer hierarchy, where the widow drops to the bottom. According to God's definition, she is right up there with everyone else. Widowhood does not downsize her God-given responsibilities or demote her from her exalted image bearer calling. There's a kingdom to build, vast enemy territory to reclaim. With a task this size, God is not about to sign off on any *ezer*-warrior's retirement or leave of absence. Whether she realizes it or not, Naomi is mission-critical to God's purposes for the world. She remains on active duty for him.

God's high view of the widow, and by implication of all women, is borne out in both the Old Testament and the New. Those hair-raising Old Testament warnings[13] that God's prophets aimed at those who neglected or mistreated the widow are strong statements of her significance in God's eyes.[14] His eye is on the widow and his ear is acutely tuned in to her cries. She is God's emissary. Any slight of her is a personal affront to God, an insult to his kingdom.

In the New Testament Jesus consistently treated widows with the same high regard he offered to others. He proved wholly uncooperative when his followers urged him to turn away determined mothers with small children, badgering beggars, and female outcasts—the so-called little people of society—or when others wanted him to treat them harshly. He went out of his way to attend to their needs and defended them against their accusers. Often he exalted people regarded as nuisances to the level of role models for the men who followed him.

Jesus made what is perhaps the most striking statement of the value of a widow when he was dying. Most biblical scholars believe that by the time Jesus reached adulthood, his own mother was a widow. If ever there was a time when a man might be forgiven for failing to notice a widow's sufferings and tears, surely it was when Jesus was being crucified. Yet right in the midst of being tortured, his heart goes out to her. In an act of exquisite compassion and esteem, the suffering Jesus transfers his responsibilities as her eldest son and protector to his beloved disciple John. To Mary he says, "Dear woman, here is your son," and to John, "Here is your mother." To which the apostle John adds this tender epilogue, "From that time on, this disciple took her into his home" (John 19:26–27). Jesus' words reveal God's heart for women and their significance in his sight.

A woman's high calling as God's image bearer renders her *incapable* of insignificance, no matter what has gone wrong in her life or how much she has lost. Even if her community shoves her aside, turns a deaf ear to the sound of her voice, or regards her as invisible—even if she is forced into a passive role in the community—she remains vital to God's purposes and is a solid contributor anyway. She simply cannot be stopped.

With God as her ally, the widow turns the tables on the culture. Instead of simply being a person in need, she emerges as someone with a lot to offer. The widow is an indispensable source of wisdom to God's people. A megawatt searchlight in God's hand, she casts a glaring light on a community, exposing the true state of her neighbors' hearts. Scripture contradicts the culture's perception of her as needy and voiceless by portraying her more accurately as a generous provider for others and as a spokesperson for God. The Bible compels us to make a complete U-turn in our thinking about the widow.

THE WIDOW TEACHES WISDOM

In ancient times, the widow moved through the community embodying a vital message for God's people. She didn't even have to open her mouth. The identifying garments that stamped a woman as a widow also transformed her into a living icon of wisdom, a vivid reminder that for everyone there is "a time to be born *and* a time to die" (Ecclesiastes 3:2, emphasis added). Like a roadside memorial commemorating the victim of an automobile crash, she possessed the power to direct the thoughts of her complacent fellow citizens to ultimate matters of life and death (at least for a moment).

Death, a certainty for all of us, is not a popular topic of conversation these days. There's a sense of unreality in the idea of death until it leaps out and invades our lives in some deeply personal way. Even when we are confronted with reminders of death's inevitability for all of us, we are not inclined to linger. It's easy to tell ourselves that the sorrow we read on the widow's face and in the wilted flowers beside the road belong to someone else. Our culture keeps its distance from death and prefers instead to dwell on happier matters. Consequently we skip whole chapters in the book of wisdom that drive us into the safe arms of Jesus and inform us how to live for him today. The widow calls us back.

The Widow Exposes Us

The book of Ruth divides the human race between the haves and the have-nots, the powerful and the weak, those with resources and those who are empty. Naomi and Ruth are card-carrying members of the have-nots. The issue at hand is not whether the local welfare system is adequate, but what God's people will do with their advantages, power, and resources.[15]

This story also divides the world between male and female. And while the disparity between men and women in our culture may not be as extreme as in other cultures, it nevertheless still exists. In this world, being born female can still be a risk. In subsequent chapters, we will explore this male/female component, for the narrator is clearly putting on the table the subject of what men will do with their advantages over women.

The widow represents vast numbers of human beings in the world who are disadvantaged—putting before us the perpetual question of whether we will hoard our blessings or open our hearts and hands to others. The widow is and has always been a litmus test to measure how much theology we've truly absorbed and how much is just talk. She in her need draws from us what we were created to give.

Amazingly, the widow practices what she preaches, for no matter what her neighbors think, God has a redemptive view of her. He retrieves this rejected woman from the margins of society and puts her on the front lines for his kingdom. This fits with who she truly is, for as God's image bearer, ruling and subduing are in her bones. The widow's proactive efforts prove we need her, just as badly as she needs us.

THE NEEDY ONE PROVIDES

The prophet Elijah survived a stretch of famine in Israel through the surprising generosity of an impoverished widow in Zarephath, who, with her young son, was facing starvation. As a matter of fact, when Elijah showed up, she and her son were down to their last small meal. In a courageous, selfless act of faith, she fed God's prophet from her meager supply of flour and oil before taking care of her child and herself.[16]

In the Jerusalem temple, Jesus noticed a poor widow dropping her last small coins into the treasury. Humanly speaking, it wasn't much. But in Jesus' eyes, her gift was extravagant, put wealthier givers to shame, and earned her the honor of his praise in the Gospels.[17] Scholars rightly point out how Jesus' commendation transforms the widow's reputation, for "she is not presented as an object of sympathy but of admiration."[18] She is a role model for all believers.

In his letters, Paul promotes earthshaking views of women that fly in the face of human culture. He speaks in radical ways of the single woman, most of whom in his day were widows. According to the apostle, a woman alone is neither incomplete nor needy, but an *asset* to God's people. Although she is free to remarry, he believes she will be "happier if she stays as she is" (1 Corinthians 7:39–40). His high view of single women in no way disparaged men or marriage, but simply reflected what he found to be true in his own life—that singles are unencumbered with family concerns and can therefore live "in undivided devotion to the Lord" (1 Corinthians 7:32–35). It also conveys Paul's conviction that women are indispensable in advancing the gospel of Christ.

Instead of viewing the "lack" of a husband as a deficiency that needs to be explained (and also remedied), as many Christians think today, Paul equates singleness with greater freedom to serve God and a path to rich satisfaction. Instead of seeing a husband as a woman's salvation, he rightly points to Jesus as the true source of every woman's fulfillment. It would be interesting to see how it would transform the experience of single women in the life of the church today, and how the church's reputation might improve with women outside the church if we actually embraced Paul's liberating teaching regarding women—if we prized, equipped, and mobilized them for the kingdom as he did.

Officially, the New Testament church at an early stage took seriously their responsibility for widows who lacked family or other resources. The office of deacon was instituted initially to address this pressing need.[19] However, these woman were not always on the receiving end, but gave of themselves in ministry to the church in a variety of ways. Paul describes the ministering widow as "well known for her good deeds, such as bringing up children, showing hospitality, washing the feet of the saints, helping those in trouble and devoting herself to all kinds of good deeds" (1 Timothy 5:10). Some believe widows "made charitable and pastoral house calls and taught younger women 'what is good.'"[20] Although we don't know a lot of details about the order of widows, "it is clear from the pastoral letters that an office for older women not only existed in the church but was large and active enough to require detailed regulation."[21]

THE "SILENT ONE" FINDS HER VOICE

Ironically, the Scriptures memorialize a number of widows who are best known for using their voices. We'll skip over Naomi and Ruth for the time being, although their voices will be heard in the Bethlehem community too. Even Jesus spoke of the widow in ways that affirmed the power of her voice. Consider the parable he told of the widow who, without legal counsel or an appointed court representative, badgered an unjust judge—literally wore him down—until he caved in to her demands. Technically, this widow had no voice or rights. That didn't stop her from fighting for justice. She courageously and boldly used her voice, refusing to be victimized or to give up until the judge conceded to her demands.[22]

Then there was the eighty-four-year-old *prophetess* Anna—an elderly, childless widow whose voice we will never forget. Widowed seven years into her marriage, she was a familiar figure in the temple, where she "worshiped night and day, fasting and praying." After her meeting with the infant Jesus and his parents, she was among the first to proclaim the gospel of Jesus—in the temple, no less. As Luke relates, "she gave thanks to God and *spoke* about the child to all who were looking forward to the redemption of Jerusalem" (Luke 2:38, emphasis added). Thurston highlights Anna's significance when she notes, "Luke at the end of the Gospel gives women the task of proclaiming Jesus' resurrection (Luke 24:8–10). Here at the beginning a woman proclaims Jesus' advent. Anna is the first evangelist."[23]

From Naomi to Now

When Naomi arrived in Bethlehem, she may have felt like a useless piece of driftwood that had washed up on the beach—a relic of a bygone golden era, a woman who had outlived her usefulness. In God's eyes, she was still on active duty and the treasure of his heart. Her story has purpose written all over it, although the signals she receives from the culture and from her own heart tell her otherwise. She is unaware of the fact that, instead of setting her aside, God is readying her for a strategic kingdom mission.

God's message for the widow hits home for all of us—whether we land with Naomi in the 90 percent of women who end up living alone or we live out our days basking in the love of our husbands and families. In a way, all of us can identify with the widow from time to time—those low moments when we are left out or don't fit in, when we have the bitter taste of rejection in our mouths, when we think we are forgotten or that our purpose has expired. Through the widow we come to understand who we are at the core of our being. We can remain confident that whatever happens, we always have a God-given mission and are part of the big things God is doing in this world.

Both Naomi and Ruth are living evidence of this. A broken Naomi returns to her homeland, convinced that God is against her and she doesn't matter anymore. Yet already God has moved Ruth to levels of loyal love for Naomi that are truly radical and speak volumes about her mother-in-law's great value. Even Bethlehem will be unable to ignore her. Before the story is over, God will mobilize the entire village on Naomi's behalf, and she will discover she still has vital contributions to make.

Ruth the Moabitess arrives in Bethlehem with several strikes against her. She is female, foreign, barren, and widowed—all reasons to consider her undesirable. Yet she is not undesirable in God's eyes. He has just carried out a successful rescue operation to reach into Moab and bring her out and into the community of his people. Through her subsequent bold actions, she becomes a catalyst for new levels of godliness and justice in the community. Ultimately, she makes the short list of Israelite matriarchs named in the royal line of Jesus—a well-deserved honor.[24]

God doesn't exile the widow to the margins of our Bible. He *features* her in the central story of redemption. If the book of Ruth is to be believed, he doesn't retire the disconnected woman from active duty; he recruits her to a leading role in the unfolding of his purposes. He holds his people accountable for securing justice for the widow, yet doesn't define her exclusively in terms of lack. Far from being a burden, the widow makes significant kingdom contributions and is someone God's people need.

"Can This Be Elois?"

If anyone had a right to think her usefulness was over, it was Elois Godfrey. The last time I saw Elois, she was parked in a wheelchair at the end of a nursing home corridor with an oxygen tube in her nose—neither the condition nor the location where anyone would expect powerful kingdom activity to take place. It was two days before Christmas, but I was not in the Christmas mood. I was in a hurry—frazzled with too little time and dozens of unfinished items on my holiday to-do list. How was I ever going to get everything done by Christmas?

As I drove near the nursing home, I battled opposing pressures to get on with my list and the thought that Elois probably wasn't having a good day either. Despite my frustrations, I decided to pay Elois a call intending to minister to her and brighten her day. I never dreamed this would be our last visit or that Elois would turn things around—that instead of ministering to her, she would minister to me. The clock was winding down for her. Although neither of us knew it at the time, she only had forty-eight hours to go.

In her prime, Elois was a schoolteacher, a musician, a poet, and an avid golfer. She was in her eighties when she and her walker made their way into our church. She never married, although even after her ninetieth birthday she insisted she was "still looking." She possessed an uncanny ability to worm her way into people's affections, a skill she used with great effect on all of us. People in my church loved her and surrounded her with care.

That day in the nursing home, Elois had serious matters on her mind. Lately, she had been complaining a lot. Who could blame her? Her health was deteriorating. She longed to be back with all of her friends at church instead of stuck in a nursing home. Two other women shared her room—one roommate was gravely ill and a second insisted on keeping the light and the television on all the time. With her usual frankness Elois recited her complaints to me. I could certainly understand why she was upset. Mid-sentence she caught herself up short and stopped. Then, as though she had forgotten I was sitting there, she began to remind herself, "I'm forgetting God is here. I'm not living for his purpose." We sat in silence for a moment, processing her words as she resolved to stop thinking about herself and to reach out to the people around her.

Even now that she is gone, those words keep replaying in my head. With time running out and her mobility severely restricted,

Elois still had a mission. She was God's image bearer to the end, doing God's work and, even without realizing it, speaking for him to me.

God's purposes for Naomi haven't expired either. Sooner than she ever imagined, she will be refreshed by his love, savoring his goodness and discovering he has more for her to do. A great awakening is coming for Naomi. But before we see what turns her around, there's another voice we need to hear. The barren woman has a message for us.

Branded a failure as a woman because of her inability to conceive, she has deep reasons to wonder if God is good for her when he denies her the very longings he implanted in her heart. Next, we turn our attention to the infertile woman to find out where her wrestlings lead and how God is intensely at work where he seems most absent. What does the barren woman have to teach us?

DISCUSSION QUESTIONS

1. What thoughts or fears cross your mind when you hear the statistic projecting that nine out of ten women will spend some part of their lives as widows?

2. What challenges have you or others you know faced as solitary women?

3. What are the similarities and differences between Job and Naomi?

4. How do Naomi's losses create a worst-case scenario in which to probe God's heart for us and our value as kingdom builders?

5. How do the widows of Vrindavan shed light on your understanding of Naomi's and Ruth's loss of value in their culture and the dangers that lay ahead for them?

6. What defines a woman's value before God, and how does his view of us differ from how the world defines and values us and how we see ourselves?

7. Describe an example in the Gospels that reflects Jesus' countercultural views of women. How did he go against the ancient culture?

8. How does your calling as image bearer shield you from losing your identity and ensure that God's mission for you remains intact, even when life turns out differently than you hoped?

Chapter Three

WISDOM GLEANED
FROM EMPTY ARMS

There are two kinds of women in this world—those who are mothers and those who are not.

Although in this day and age some women are child free by choice and don't feel their identity or status as women suffers at all, throughout history a woman's identity and significance have teetered perilously on the pivot point of whether or not she can successfully give birth. Even today, in the minds of many, giving birth to a child is a defining event for a woman—her rite of passage into womanhood. As one woman told me, "Having a baby validates our womanhood"—a notion that creates enormous inner turmoil for the woman who fails to conceive or to bring a baby to term.

Five years before I met my husband, when doctors diagnosed me with endometriosis (a major culprit in the infertility epidemic), I knew I was in trouble. Five years into marriage—following a battery of medical procedures, surgeries, high doses of pain medication, and many disappointments—I was once again wheeled into a Philadelphia operating room. On the other side of surgery, I awoke to the news that I would never bear a child. With the sharp finality of a guillotine, my battle against infertility was over.

Nurses told me they usually have to sedate women who get that kind of news. Support came to me from another source. This was one of those moments in my marriage when I saw fresh evidence that my husband didn't value me for my childbearing abilities. He valued me for myself. Frank's response to the surgeon's devastating news freed me from being defined by that surgery and saved me from plummeting in grief. As far as he was concerned, the God who loved us as much as ever had closed this door. This surgery was one of many painful reminders that we were not in charge of the journey we were on, but we held onto the belief that somehow God's good purposes for us were bound up in everything that happened along the way.

I can't explain why I felt the safety net beneath me that time and why so many other disappointments both before and since have triggered a crisis of faith. I only know that it wasn't the end of the world—and it wasn't the end of me. We helped each other trust God and felt a growing sense of expectation over where he might lead us next, now that this path was closed. It wasn't until two years later, after we moved to California, that I was hit by what I had lost.

In the interim, God unexpectedly overturned the outcome of my surgery by blessing us with a beautiful baby girl. As Frank often says, "God has more than one way of making families," and we were proof of that. We lived with a deep sense of God's hand in weaving our three lives together. It was one of the richest times of our lives.

Several months later we relocated to Southern California where, at a faculty picnic shortly after our arrival, I was sitting with a group of young wives I had just met. One woman was days away from delivering her first baby, so it was natural for the conversation to turn to babies and childbirth and even more natural, I suppose, for them to be curious about me since I was the only mother in the group. I never saw it coming, the question that caught me up short: "So ... what was childbirth like for you?"

As if on cue, everyone turned to me. It was a moment I will never forget. I had a story to tell—a miraculous one that still stuns me with God's unexpected goodness. It wasn't the story they wanted to hear. Not only did their sudden interest in me evaporate, I felt discredited as a woman. I had nothing to contribute to their conversation, which they resumed without me. I have since learned to excuse myself when women start sharing their delivery room experiences.

THE DESPERATE QUEST FOR SONS

Attitudes I bumped into that day—that made me feel deficient as a woman—are mild compared to what infertile women face in Third World countries where childlessness reaches a whole new decibel of pain. Not only do women face the sorrow of personal disappointment (along with the disadvantages of being unable to afford or access the latest medical technologies that might improve their chances of a successful pregnancy), they come under fierce pressure from in-laws to conceive and suffer frightening consequences if they do not.

I asked a Tanzanian friend what happens in his country when a woman fails to conceive. He answered gravely, "She's in trouble. Her husband has grounds for divorce." He went on to explain that the problem extends beyond my question, for a woman is not simply under pressure to bear children, she must give birth to *sons*. In patriarchal cultures, sons are prized. Daughters are not. A daughter leaves to build another man's house. But a son will carry on his father's name, build his father's house, and inherit his father's wealth. A man *must* have a son. If his wife lets him down in this, his family will press him to discard her—either by divorce or polygamy—and find another wife who can produce a son. His relatives depend on him to perpetuate the family name and solidify them economically for another generation. He depends on his wife to save his honor and preserve his name. If she fails, he will do whatever it takes to fulfill his duty and protect himself.

The same desperate quest for sons dominates the landscape of the Bible. Hannah didn't pray for any child. She wept and pleaded for a son. Jacob's wives, Leah and Rachel, were in an all-out war to see who could produce the greatest number of sons for their husband. Dinah, the one daughter mentioned, is Leah's disappointing seventh child—the girl who cheated her mother out of the crowning achievement of producing seven sons. When the aging Elizabeth finally conceives, she recalls her decades of barrenness as a time of public "disgrace" or "shame" from which God has finally delivered her (Luke 1:25). Her words reveal the inescapable stigma and mental anguish attached to childlessness.

This was the world of Ruth and Orpah too, and, in the words of my Tanzanian friend, both of them were "in trouble." Although the narrator doesn't disclose the details, given what we know of the ancient society, it is a fair assumption that after ten years of their Moabite wives' barrenness, both Mahlon and Kilion were weighing their options. The ancient motto was "Family survival at all cost." The barren wife was first to pay.

There is much about this value system that ought to keep us awake at night. As a daughter, I find it chilling to think that had I been born in another culture, my birth would have been a defeat for my father and potentially dangerous for my mother, especially if I had been her firstborn. It's hard to imagine my parents throwing me out with the garbage to die of exposure, but that might have happened too.

As a wife, I doubt there is a sedative strong enough to dull the pain if, instead of joining me in my postsurgery struggle, Frank had served me with divorce papers or announced he was adding a second wife. I didn't have to face any of these shattering consequences. My husband never considered blaming or abandoning me and loved me more than ever.

For Naomi and Ruth, however, the world suddenly grew hostile and unsafe when the combined forces of widowhood and childlessness dislodged them from the security of husband and home. The barren woman joins the widow in the margins of society. She just got there through a different door. For women in either category (or both, as was the case for Naomi and Ruth) displacement is a sure, short road to poverty—or worse.

THE GOSPEL OVERTURNS THE CULTURE

God is not silent on these matters. In both Old and New Testaments the transforming nature of the gospel shines through, elevating women to heights of significance and dignity unheard of in human cultures but perfectly consistent with our calling as God's image bearers.

Contrary to the ancient culture's tendency to discard barren women as useless members of society, God refuses to drop them from his script. Instead of banishing them to the margins of his story, he resolutely moves them to the forefront and recruits them for pivotal roles in the history of redemption. The book of Ruth is a prime example. Here, two childless widows become the lead figures in a biblical book. As often happens in the Bible, the storyline narrows from a wider national tapestry to a slender thread where one woman's choices, initiatives, and leadership have global repercussions and work good for all of us. Both Ruth and Naomi's actions rise from the mundane, the ordinary, and the marginal to what is rightly deemed to be earthshaking and central.

According to Scripture, Naomi's wrestlings with God are weighty matters, not to be brushed aside as a matter of female disposition or minimized as some kind of hormonal episode. The Bible takes her seriously and expects us to do the same, for our own sakes as much as to honor her. And the simple everyday battles Ruth is fighting to put food on the table and to rescue a dying family are not private matters of little concern to anyone else. The redemption of humanity hangs in the balance. The line Ruth is fighting to save "just happens" to be the royal line of Israel—the ancestors of the Messiah. Ironically, God's purposes for humanity are riding on the shoulders of two women the world believes have lost their ability to contribute.

When the gospel reaches its fullness in Jesus, it overflows with good news for women. Just as Jesus overturned the trading tables in the temple, he also overthrows humanity's habit of devaluing of women and girls. When a twelve-year-old girl lay dying, Jesus could have turned a blind eye. After all, he was busy with his disciples and a large crowd of adults. Besides, aren't little girls disposable? Yet, Jesus dropped everything he was doing, left the crowd behind, and rushed to her bedside to bring her back to life—making an emphatic statement of her true significance. En route, he paused to heal and restore an outcast woman who had lost twelve precious childbearing years because of hemorrhaging that rendered her ceremonially unclean. She was an untouchable in the community, as well as to her husband. Jesus' compassionate, affirming actions toward her created a shocking display of how out of step he was with his culture—a society where men regularly praised God that they hadn't been born female.

Insofar as barren women are concerned, the significance of their contributions in advancing God's redemptive purposes goes well beyond the eventual reversal of their barrenness and the birthing of important sons. In these deeply personal struggles, God was shaping souls, equipping his daughters for greater kingdom responsibilities, and revealing facets of his character that, oddly enough, were actually illumined by their barrenness. From the depths of their denied longings for a child, these women emerge as wise teachers for God's people.

THE "SILENT" EPIDEMIC

Today, some call infertility "the silent epidemic" because (at least at first) only the couple and their physician know. "Silent" hardly captures the experience of these sorrowful women in biblical times. Their intimate secrets are trumpeted like tabloid headlines for everyone to see. "Now Sarai was barren; she had no children" (Genesis 11:30) are lines Abraham's wife Sarah would have struck from Genesis if she had been the editor. Hannah's private torment—exacerbated by polygamy—is exposed in a factual statement that reads like a census bureau statistic: "Peninnah had children, but Hannah had none" (1 Samuel 1:2).

Their stories are captured in a few terse sentences, which can disguise the fact that these wrenching ordeals dragged on for years. Sarah and Elizabeth suffered for decades before their childbearing years expired. Rebekah waited for twenty long years before giving birth to twins.[1] By then, her contemporaries were cuddling their grandsons. Rachel's husband, Jacob, fathered eleven children—ten sons and one daughter—by three other women before Rachel's day finally arrived.

The Bible broadcasts situations where, frantic over their predicament, barren women lose control and speak or act in shameful ways. Sarah heartlessly commandeers Hagar, her handmaid, as a surrogate mother. Leah and Rachel treat their maids with similar disregard and bargain callously with each other over bedroom privileges with their shared husband, Jacob. "Give me children, or I'll die," is Rachel's agonizing cry (Genesis 30:1). Marital tensions explode; harsh words are exchanged—giving us a small taste of the terrible desperation these women experienced.

In contrast, Ruth's infertility is discreetly camouflaged between the lines of her story where a lot of readers pass over it. Even those who notice tend not to take her troubles seriously, especially given the fact that in the final chapter Ruth conceives and gives birth to a son. Modern readers are inclined to reduce her barrenness to a necessary but almost incidental plot element—a fleeting problem that sets up the necessity for her second marriage to Boaz. But if our own experiences and those of other barren women in the Bible tell us anything, barrenness took a toll on Ruth too, and she felt the shame of her failure. Ironically, this private, easy-to-miss detail is one of the most important things we can know about Ruth, and we need to bring it along with us through the remainder of her story.

A "FEMALE PROBLEM"

Throughout history the finger of blame for infertility has consistently (albeit unjustly) pointed at women, and they have felt the bitter consequences. Women are also wrongly blamed for the sex of a child. Only in the last century has medical science finally set the record straight, when scientists determined that the causes of infertility are actually shared pretty evenly between men and women and that a child's sex is not determined by the mother after all, but by the father's "X" and "Y" chromosomes. Who knows how many women have been condemned and punished for a "crime" they didn't commit?

In Ruth's day these findings were not available. If you had asked anyone living at the time, including Ruth herself, they would uniformly place the failure to conceive squarely and solely on her shoulders. She alone bore the label "barren." Mahlon was exempt. Even if Mahlon also contributed to their childlessness, as some believe, in the final episode of her story we are told that "the LORD enabled her to conceive" (Ruth 4:13), a clear announcement that God directly intervened to reverse her barrenness. We may not typically think of Ruth as infertile, but she belongs to the impressive company of Israel's barren matriarchs nonetheless.

The fact that barrenness was viewed as a female problem and that a husband had options to resolve the problem for himself meant the barren woman generally went through this struggle alone. Barrenness ceased to be a problem for Abraham, Jacob, or Elkanah, who fathered children by other women, but the sufferings of Sarah, Rachel, and Hannah persisted unabated. While a husband celebrated another wife's conception or delivery of a son, his childless wife was left to deal alone with why God had left her out. Barrenness was *her* problem.

These decidedly female moments in the Bible narrow our focus to a woman's relationship with God. The isolating nature of her sufferings meant a woman could no longer lean on someone else's theology. Pressed by circumstances and intensely personal pain, she must cultivate her own relationship with God, probe his heart, and think for herself, sometimes for the first time in her life.

INCONCEIVABLE

Today we use a lot of fancy medical terminology (like polycystic ovarian syndrome, endometriosis, abnormal hormone levels, scarring and blockage of fallopian tubes) to explain why women can't get pregnant. In the ancient biblical world, however, diagnosticians skipped over secondary causes to focus attention on the root cause of barrenness. Medical charts of barren women in the Bible bore this cryptic notation: "The LORD had closed her womb."[2]

It's easy to read blunt statements like this with the same breezy detachment we devote to a restaurant menu. Yet if we stop to think about it, it's hard to imagine a more troubling statement for the woman who is begging God for a child and watching her last few chances for a family slip away. We want the Bible to tell us that God loves us so dearly he cannot bear to see us suffer; we want him to stand *between* us and adversity. When we're in trouble, we want to know he's on his way at warp speed — a divine paramedic laden with soothing balm for our aching souls and the healing power to fix what's wrong. We want him to sort out scrambled hormone levels, clear blocked fallopian tubes, and bring on the blessed event we crave. It's quite a shock to discover God is here already, that he's the one who stopped the action and turned out the lights.

I find it remarkable that biblical writers don't quietly stash this disturbing disclosure away in a closet — a dark family secret we don't want anyone else to know and where I won't have to look at it either. This was what Naomi feared all along — that God wasn't on her side, but was working against her. It's one thing to know this behind-the-scenes piece of information once the stories turn out happily, as they ultimately do for Sarah, Rachel, Ruth, and Hannah. But a lot of infertile women don't end up with a baby in their arms, and so for them, the issue isn't quite so simple.

Out of his own unending sorrow over the death of his son, Christian philosopher Nicholas Wolterstorff captures the confusion that comes from knowing the God who loves us is in the picture, and still things are turning out badly for us. Wolterstorff sounds a lot like Naomi:

> I am at an impasse, and you, O God, have brought me here.…
> From my earliest days, I believed in you. I shared in the life of
> your people: in their prayers, in their work, in their songs.…

For me your yoke was easy. On me your presence smiled. Noon has darkened.... And where are you in this darkness?... Or is it not your absence in which I dwell but your elusive troubling presence?[3]

WISDOM'S GLEANINGS

I can't explain why God closes a woman's womb or why Naomi and Job suffered so much. To be honest, I don't have answers for my own heartaches. Still, we can glean wisdom from these women's struggles with God—wisdom that will come to our aid whenever we reach a similar impasse with God.

One of the first nuggets of wisdom we gain from the barren woman is something we so easily forget: *we never have all the facts.* We can guess all we like at why certain things go wrong, why one woman is happily fertile and another woman helplessly watches the years slip away without a single conception despite tears and prayers and a relentless faith in God. If these ancient sufferers tell us anything, it is that God's ways are mysterious. He isn't obligated to explain himself, and often doesn't. I'm not even convinced (as some are) that he is waiting for me at heaven's gates with explanations for the list of unanswered questions I accumulated here on earth.

Even when we can pinpoint "something good" that came out of a tragedy, it *never* balances out what we have lost. How could anything compensate Naomi for the loss of her husband and sons? What could possibly make up for Job's losses of his children and his workers? Can any trade-off fill the void in a woman's heart when her longings for a child go unanswered and her husband rejects her and turns to another woman?

No, the balance sheet *always* comes up short when we try to confine God in some delicate balancing act where the physical blessings we receive match and somehow overcome our losses. We live in the realm of faith, and that means trusting God for who he is and not because things equal out or we have satisfying answers to our questions. Faith may want answers, but somehow it is able to survive without them. That's at least part of the wisdom the barren woman imparts to us.

We also learn from barren women that God uses suffering to open our eyes to see more of him than we would under rosier conditions. At some point, we grow weary of tears and our thrashings die down. We are quiet—not because we've gotten answers to our troubling questions, but because we are spent. When we are in pain, we may get the sense that God has vanished from our lives. In truth, the opposite has happened. *God meets us in our pain.* The death of his son drew Wolterstorff limping into a deeper, almost frightening connection with God. "The world has a hole in it now," he sorrowed. "I shall look at the world through tears. Perhaps I shall see things that dry-eyed I could not see."[4]

Suffering is a sacred meeting place between God and his child, where faith is fighting to survive and God's goodness comes into question. Throughout biblical history, God used infertility to pull his distressed daughters aside and engage them at a deeper level. Through suffering, God led them on a descent into darkness, doubt, and despair—foreboding, mysterious places we would never go by choice, but where God inevitably leads us. In the darkness we strain our eyes, searching for signs of him. We listen intently for the slightest movement that will tell us he is near. The barren women tell us he is here—in this dark place, in the middle of the mess, and in the depths of our despair. This is where childless women discovered things about God they would not have seen "dry-eyed" and where they came to acknowledge a staggering level of dependence on him that was informed by their barrenness.

Perhaps the biggest (and most unexpected) gift these barren women give us is a glimpse in *their* mirror to see our own faces reflected back. Their barrenness is not just a connecting point with other women who happen to be infertile too. At a fundamental level, their barrenness relates to all of us. So how does barrenness relate to everyone?

The Facts of Life

I remember the day my schoolteacher shuffled the boys in our class into another room so the school nurse could explain the facts of life to the girls and brace us for changes puberty was soon to bring. Fortunately, most of our mothers already had that talk with us. When God explains the facts of life to his children, however, he doesn't divide the boys and girls into separate groups. He wants us all to be in on the discussion. And he doesn't recruit the school nurse for the job either. He appoints the barren woman.

The central fact of life she wants to teach us—one that God himself etched in her aching soul—is that God alone is the life giver. A woman's repeated failures to conceive convince her of the fact that she cannot create a life. This is not new revelation, but reconnects us to one of the oldest truths we know, a truth whose roots go back to antiquity. One of the biggest messages of creation is that all life finds its source in God. God "breathed into [Adam's] nostrils the breath of life, and the man became a living being" (Genesis 2:7).

So often we think women who struggle with infertility are exceptions to the rule. If the statistics are correct, most women don't have a problem. The barren woman begs to differ. She is not an exception. She is the rule. We are all poor souls in need of a miracle, and we cannot get along just fine on our own. Every once in a while, God pulls back the curtain and shows us how things really work. He does that with the barren woman who shows us that *we are all infertile*. Every child conceived is a miracle—and while we all acknowledge this to be true at one level, it's easy to forget when conception and birth happen according to our timetable.

The barren woman grounds us in reality, for her teachings go beyond the delivery room, encompassing everything in life. She acknowledges God to be Lord of the womb—of *every* womb—- and of every other sphere of life. We are not the masters of our own destinies. We are called to plan and strategize, to work and live active lives, to attempt things that are beyond us and tackle challenges that stretch us to the limit. Yet the outcome of our efforts, even our ability to exert ourselves, is always in God's hands. Both Naomi and Ruth discover this when they arrive in Bethlehem and simply try to survive. Ruth will make the most (and presses the boundaries) of the limited opportunities before her. But she cannot create her own success. She is powerless without God's help. Author Phillip Yancey agrees:

As adults we like to pay our own way, live in our own houses, make our own decisions, rely on no outside help. We look down upon those who live off welfare or charity. Faced with an unexpected challenge, we seek out "self-help" books. All the while we are systematically sealing off the heart attitude most desirable to God and most descriptive of our true state in the universe. "Apart from me you can do nothing," Jesus told his disciples, a plain fact that we conspire to deny.[5]

We are all impotent and in need of God's help when conceiving new life or tackling some difficult task. But there is another place where impotency confronts us.

SECOND STAGE INFERTILITY

In the Grandview Cemetery in Fort Collins, Colorado, a small, forgotten grave lies nestled in among a circle of large stone markers commemorating the lives and deaths of several adults. A few years ago I paid a visit to this grassy unmarked site. Here was the tear-soaked ground where my paternal grandmother wept and where she buried her eight-day-old firstborn, William Granville Custis Jr.—a tiny victim of the 1919 influenza epidemic. But for my grandmother, the weeping didn't stop here. Seven pregnancies later, she was still shedding tears over some of her children, not because their lives were in any physical danger, but because of her inability to reproduce herself spiritually in them.

My godly grandmother encountered a problem that can be traced back as far as Adam and Eve. Although our first parents didn't die physically the moment their lips touched the fruit, there were two fatalities in the garden at that moment, for both of them experienced spiritual death and the symptoms surfaced instantly. Now, instead of seeking and savoring God's fellowship as they once did, "they hid from the LORD God among the trees of the garden" (Genesis 3:8). Then, confronted by their sin, they made excuses and shifted blame. They displayed no signs of remorse, no inclination to repent, no pulse of spiritual life. If a coroner had arrived on the scene, he would have pronounced them both spiritually dead and hauled them off in body bags. Instead, they reproduced after their own kind, generating a world full of people whose bodies are alive, but whose hearts are lifeless toward God.

The apostle Paul raises the subject of barrenness to the level of a theological teaching when he brings up Sarah and Abraham in Romans. This is not a sidebar for couples who struggle to have children. It is the centerpiece of Paul's discussion of how, against hope, God births each of us into the family of faith—the family of the aged Abraham.[6] God chose a hopelessly infertile elderly couple when he wanted to build a great nation. Humanly speaking, it was doubly a lost cause from the start, for Abraham's "body was as good as dead" and "Sarah's womb was also dead" (Romans 4:19). Yet Abraham believed "God had power to do what he had promised" (Romans 4:21). God chose Sarah and Abraham to remind us that every Christian born into God's family is a miracle.

When we preach the gospel to unbelievers, whether they are our children, a neighbor, or a coworker, we are talking to the dead. Ezekiel preached to a field of dry bones, but only God could bring those bones to life. It takes God's mega-voltage resurrection power to awaken a human soul from death to life. No amount of persuasion, perseverance, loving-kindness, or proven evangelistic techniques can overcome the grip of death and breathe life into the human soul, although God regularly employs all of these methods and more in the birthing process. The same high-voltage resurrection power that released Jesus from the tomb works every time a sinner turns to Christ.[7] Every child born into God's family is a miracle.

Resurrection power took hold of Ruth on the road from Moab to Bethlehem. There's no other way to explain what happened to her. What were the chances that she would turn to God after seeing all the bad things that had happened to Naomi? And what a marvel that God chose Naomi (who had nothing good to say about him and was actually trying to send Ruth away) to be the evangelist! I love to contemplate the irony of it all—the improbability of Ruth's choice and the unlikelihood of Naomi being the one to show the way.

It reassures me that God will work through me too, even though I am spiritually infertile, even when I (like Naomi) am discouraged and wrestling with doubts, even when I sin and fail and say all the wrong things. The simple, encouraging truth that keeps me going is the fact that God's preferred method of saving the lost is to work through us. According to Paul, "we carry this precious Message around in the unadorned clay pots of our ordinary lives. That's to prevent anyone from confusing God's incomparable power with us" (2 Corinthians 4:7, The Message). God's resurrection power is at work through powerless people to bring dead souls to life. He always works that way.

O LITTLE TOWN OF BETHLEHEM

When Naomi and Ruth gathered up their bundles and resumed the journey to Bethlehem, they also picked up their theology —- beliefs about God forged in the crucible of affliction. Despair and hope are traveling side by side. What they believe will show up in how they live.

Down the road lay Bethlehem. Does anyone there have an inkling of what is heading their way? Two widows who at first sight look like they have nothing to offer and will be a drain on village resources. No one is bracing for the powerful tremors that are about to shake up their sleepy little community when the two Elimelech widows arrive with their broken-down lives and God's resurrection power at work in them.

By the time the story is over, all Bethlehem—from the field hands to the city elders—will feel the impact of their presence. But for now, village residents go about their ordinary business without any forewarning that the little town of Bethlehem is about to be jolted out of her "deep and dreamless sleep." The people of God will look back upon this day as a turning point in Israel's history.

The narrator only gives us the slightest hint of what is in store, with the simple statement that they arrived "in Bethlehem as the barley harvest was beginning" (Ruth 1:21). This foreshadowing of better days to come is enough to make even readers who are most familiar with this story turn the page.

DISCUSSION QUESTIONS

1. Why do you think childbearing is viewed so central to our identity as women and our purpose in life?

2. Why is the pressure to conceive a son so intense in the biblical culture and in Third World cultures today?

3. How did barrenness impact the relationship between women in the Bible and God?

4. What does the barren woman teach us about God?

5. What does she teach us about ourselves?

6. How does infertility impact other areas of our lives?

7. Why does God want us to understand that we are all barren, both physically and spiritually? What difference does it make?

8. What hope can we draw from God's resurrection power in situations where we feel most powerless?

Chapter Four

BREAKING THE RULES
IN BETHLEHEM

"And ain't I a woman?"

Defiant words rang through the air at the Ohio Women's Rights Convention in 1851. The voice belonged to a tall, angular woman who was a former African slave. Sojourner Truth was publicly dismantling the notion that femininity—hers or any other woman's—-depends on delicacy or being treated like a fragile teacup.

> That man over there says that women need to be helped into carriages, and lifted over ditches, and to have the best place everywhere. Nobody ever helps me into carriages, or over mud-puddles, or gives me any best place! *And ain't I a woman?* Look at me! Look at my arm! I have ploughed and planted, and gathered into barns, and no man could head me! *And ain't I a woman?* I could work as much and eat as much as a man—when I could get it—and bear the lash as well! *And ain't I a woman?* I have borne thirteen children, and seen most all sold off to slavery, and when I cried out with my mother's grief, none but Jesus heard me! *And ain't I a woman?*[1]

Sojourner wasn't protesting chivalry toward women because she scorned gentility or disparaged the finer things in life. She was, however, challenging popular notions of what it means to be a woman. Her objections were borne from a deep inner conviction that in this broken world being a woman often means doing hard things, straining your muscles, and tackling messy problems that aren't listed in books about true femininity and may actually be repudiated by them. Sometimes God even calls us to do things that violate our personal list of what we consider "appropriate activities" for ourselves as women, but which are nevertheless a woman's calling.

Sojourner Truth was an *ezer*. For her, being a woman included sweating in the fields alongside the men; exerting physical strength to plough, plant, and harvest; fighting fierce and terrible battles for her children; and taking up unpopular causes to win justice for slaves and women. She unflinchingly entered any battle Jesus summoned her to fight and did so with every ounce of womanly strength she possessed. She believed embracing the challenges God presents can never diminish our womanhood or femininity, no matter what others (or our own inner voice) may tell us.

Sojourner Truth reminds me of Ruth. After returning to Bethlehem, the young Moabitess faced a battle that demanded more of her than she had ever been asked to give. Hunger—the enemy that drove the Elimelech family out of Bethlehem in the first place—was waiting on the doorstep when she and Naomi returned. Their situation was desperate. If they hoped to eat, Ruth must work—a task that pushed her out of the shelter of home and into the workplace where she became a common field laborer.

But the Ruth who put her foot down with Naomi back on the road to Bethlehem is the same Ruth waking up in Naomi's house after their arrival. Despite the younger widow's aching heart and her anxieties about the future, she remains as unpredictable and as capable of radical choices as ever. Passivity is not one of Ruth's strengths. To the contrary, she is decisive and proactive. No help comes from Naomi's quarter, however, for the older widow is in no frame of mind to enter into Ruth's decision. Ruth is on her own. She makes up her mind and initiates her plan. She will go to glean.[2] Her hands will be roughened by the hard work. She will toil and sweat for hours under the sweltering Judean sun for a handful of raw grain. But, like Sojourner Truth, Ruth is an *ezer*. She doesn't shrink back from what must be done, but bares her arms to the demands of today. *And ain't she a woman!*

SUSPENDING THE ACTION

This is the point in the book of Ruth where we tend to lose sight of what has happened so far. The defeats of Moab are quickly forgotten in the barley fields of Bethlehem. We set aside the miseries of the past and settle in comfortably for what promises to be a first-rate Cinderella story. The soundtrack playing in our heads modulates hopefully from the dreary minor key we've been hearing to a sprightly upbeat theme better suited to the fortuitous meeting between Boaz and Ruth that is just around the corner. These fanciful impressions cloud our vision of the real-life story unfolding and trivialize the powerful interactions playing out before us. So before we continue, we need to suspend the action to take a closer look at our two heroines and at the baggage they have brought with them from Moab.

Psychologists often tell us that the kinds of losses Naomi and Ruth have suffered—loss of a spouse, loss of a child, financial collapse, and a major move—are among the unwelcome life events that can trigger depression. Wounds inflicted by traumas of this magnitude do not easily heal, and the accompanying painful memories have remarkable staying power. If on their arrival, Naomi and Ruth passed through Bethlehem customs, a vigilant immigration officer would quickly spot cumbersome pieces of the past in their bundles—old "furniture" smuggled in from Moab that will define the décor of the rest of their lives.

We can reasonably assume that both women are battling depression. Yes, even Ruth. Both feel the gloomy pall that hangs on long after the flurry of funeral activity subsides and everyone picks up their empty casserole dishes and goes home. In the dismal aftermath, even the simple task of getting out of bed in the morning can be asking too much. It's never easy to carry on with life in a world that has been emptied of a loved one. Add to that the daunting challenges ahead of them, and reality comes into sharper focus.

Of the two, Naomi (*Mara* or "bitter" as she prefers to be called) appears less able to function. Little wonder, for her depression is compounded by her belief that Yahweh has withdrawn his love and turned against her. Hopelessness weighs a lot. Phillip Yancey understands. "Pain narrows vision," he writes. "The most private of sensations, it forces us to think of ourselves and little else."[3] Engulfed in bitterness and despair, Naomi turns inward and shuts down.

Ruth is hurting too. But while she faces the same oppressive realities, she is being reshaped by the vow she pledged to Naomi on the journey. Her vow drives her actions and informs her choices from the moment she swears loyalty to Naomi until the day the younger widow dies. We will never understand Ruth if we leave her vow behind. By her own choice she will no longer think solely of herself or live in pursuit of personal happiness. Naomi is her priority now, and Ruth will do whatever it takes to protect and provide for her demoralized mother-in-law. The gospel (even in its most primitive Old Testament form) has the power to rescue a believer from drowning in herself by moving her to think of someone else. Energized by her vow to Naomi and her newfound faith in Yahweh, Ruth turns outward and mobilizes.

A MAN OF VALOR

Resumption of the story is delayed further by the narrator, who detours unexpectedly to introduce Boaz out of sequence. Before Boaz sets foot in the story, the narrator wants us to take a good long look at the man who is about to fill the void left behind by the deaths of Elimelech, Mahlon, and Kilion. The intent, at least in part, is for us to absorb the kind of imposing man Boaz is—to examine his credentials and recognize that the man Ruth is about to encounter is anything but ordinary.

Fans of the book of Ruth have been anticipating Boaz's arrival. Here is a man possessing wealth, stature, and power. Somewhere along the line we've thrown in "handsome, eligible bachelor."

But, truthfully, there's nothing in the text to support this addition, even though it gratifies our Western appetite for romance. What the writer wants us to notice (and admire) is Boaz's sterling character, for along with wealth, rank, and power, he is presented as a man of valor.[4]

This accolade is the ancient world's equivalent of the Pulitzer Prize or the Congressional Medal of Honor. It distinguishes Boaz from other men as a champion of sorts. He is "a mighty man of power, a worthy man,"[5] a fact his subsequent actions corroborate. According to Hebrew scholars, a man of valor is "the elite warrior similar to the hero of the Homeric epic."[6] The word encompasses attributes like strength, wealth, honorable reputation, competence, and action. No one knows whether Boaz was a decorated military hero, but given Israel's frequent bloody clashes with neighboring nations during the period of the judges, that is entirely possible. We know Boaz best as a landowner, the master of the fields where much of Ruth's story takes place. He is a man with the resources, the character, and the clout to make a difference for Naomi.[7]

Boaz's impressive resume creates a startling contrast with the low rank, poverty, and vulnerability of our two heroines. If opposites attract, the three are almost certain to be drawn together. The disparities are glaring. According to Robert Hubbard, "his fullness was the counterpart to Naomi's emptiness."[8] Boaz is powerful; the women are powerless and vulnerable. He has wealth and resources; they battle poverty and hunger. His maleness comes with automatic advantages; their femaleness puts them at risk. Unlike Naomi and Ruth, who derive identity and significance from the men in their lives, Boaz stands tall on his own. In the ancient world, he holds all the cards; the women arrive empty-handed.

With the literary flair of a suspense novelist, the narrator throws in a surprise twist by linking Boaz to Naomi through Elimelech. Boaz is Elimelech's relative.[9] Both men are of the tribe of Judah and of the Ephrathite clan. Within the nation, family ties were knotted tightly and came with an extraordinary call to sacrifice. These clues set up the interaction between Boaz and

Ruth and almost certainly caused original readers of the book of Ruth to exchange knowing looks, for this information connects Boaz to King David.

Not only is Boaz a striking figure, he is also a hopeful one. Naomi's eventual discovery of his presence in their story—-especially after she learns of his generous conduct—will cause a gentle breeze of hope to blow lightly over her despairing soul. For the moment, however, Naomi and Ruth are in the dark about the imposing figure who is about to enter their story. Boaz remains a secret between the reader and the narrator, and first-time readers can only wonder how a powerful man like Boaz will treat an outsider like Ruth.

A MOMENT TO REMEMBER

Usually the moment in this episode that captures our imagination is when Boaz arrives at the field and his eyes first meet Ruth's. This is seen as the true turning point in the story—when Ruth is swept off her feet and the beautiful spirit of a woman captures the soul of a man. Now the real story begins, we muse with a smile.

But to be honest, this isn't the moment that I find the most riveting. For me the moment that changes everything and that actually signals a turn for the better in Ruth's and Naomi's fortunes is when Boaz and his workers exchange greetings. What sounds at first like a simple "Hello!" and "Good morning!"—actually puts a stake in the ground to distinguish this barley field from any other place on the planet. Greetings couched in the richly intentional language of liturgy—"The LORD be with you!" answered by "The LORD bless you!"—should cause us (and almost certainly did cause Ruth) to sit up and take notice. Expectations soar, not in anticipation of a budding romance, but of something far more earthshaking, for the speakers are openly summoning Yahweh to be present among them. In a few brief words, we are suddenly presented with a hint that by wandering into this particular barley field the grieving, impoverished, socially isolated Ruth has discovered sanctuary.

Early one Texas Sunday morning, when my husband was a young boy about the age of nine, he corralled his three younger brothers and made them scrub and dress; together they trooped down the street to the local church—the building in the block with a steeple on top. Once inside, the four boys tumbled into the back pew where they no doubt squirmed and lacked the proper church etiquette (not to mention attire) expected of young children in a worship service. Lots of people noticed them, but no one came near or spoke a word. No man reached into these young boys lives to fill a huge void with the love of a father, friend, or mentor. No woman embraced them with a warm smile and inviting words of welcome. No one answered the call to represent Jesus to these boys or viewed them through his redemptive eyes. No one imagined a future seminary president, a gifted artist and landscape architect, or four future fathers.

Put off by four scruffy little boys, adults who were there that morning were blinded and could not see past the oddity and inconvenience of four children alone in the back of the church. I wonder how four young paths might have been smoothed and spiritual journeys aided or how stuffy church people's lives might have been enriched if four small boys had found sanctuary that morning and a taste of Jesus from the love of his followers. I wonder if any of us truly grasps the power we have to rescue and bless the lives of others when we bear the name of Jesus and he is present with us.

The story turns out differently for Ruth. Boaz and his harvesters give her a staggeringly real example of Yahweh's image bearers in action. As a human being, Ruth herself has always borne the lofty identity of God's image bearer. Becoming a follower of Yahweh significantly raises the bar for her. Almost instinctively she reflects a passion and a purpose to become like him. She has already placed radical expectations on herself that she is boldly carrying out. Throughout her story, she consistently exhibits an all-or-nothing faith in Yahweh. On the road to Bethlehem, she lays down her life for her mother-in-law. Here in the barley field she will prove fearless in seeing just how far she can go as a gleaner to fulfill her vow. The seemingly innocuous greetings turn the camera lens away from Ruth and onto the recently arrived Boaz and his workers. What difference will it make for Yahweh to be present in this field? What will Ruth experience in her interactions with the Bethlehemites she encounters this day?

THE ANCIENT WELFARE SYSTEM

When Boaz woke up that morning, he had a hearty breakfast, a full agenda in front of him, and no forewarning that his life was about to change. Plans for the day included a routine trip to his barley fields to check on progress, talk to his foreman, and make sure things were running smoothly. Boaz was a man who was paying attention. Unlike many in the days of the judges, the man was meticulous in keeping God's commands both in his personal conduct and in how he ran his business.

In the fields belonging to Boaz gleaning practices were in effect. The "Gleaners Welcome" sign was posted conspicuously, in compliance with Mosaic Law. We'd expect no less from a man of such honorable reputation. This meant that his harvesters left the corners and edges of the field uncut when they harvested and that they only combed once over the field, leaving behind uncut grain and missed scraps for the poor—the widow, the orphan, and the foreigner.[10]

We have idealized images of how gleaning actually worked. We've all seen lovely pastoral paintings of gentle maidens scooping up armloads of golden grain. In reality, gleaners were often mistreated and went home hungry. A landowner might choose to keep them out or eject them if he pleased. Harvesters could get rough.[11] Unattached women were especially at risk and could be (and were) victimized. Then, of course, gleaners competed with each other. Bump into another gleaner who is stronger, more aggressive, or simply hunger-driven, and you can expect to get shoved around. Depending on conditions and attitudes in the field, Ruth could easily labor all day and not bring home enough to feed her mother-in-law and herself.

When I was on a mission trip in Central America, a missionary took the idealism out of my views of gleaning during a brief but unforgettable outing to the local garbage dump. It was a filthy place, and the stench turned my stomach. But more appalling than the odor was the sight of people—men, women, and children—- crawling over piles of rubbish like an army of ants, *gleaning* "edible" bits of trash to eat and reusable scraps of cardboard to reinforce the flimsy walls of their dilapidated shacks. I couldn't fathom eating anything in that awful place and afterward felt depressed for days. I still think of gleaners whenever I see a homeless person rummaging in the garbage outside a fast-food restaurant, scavenging for a few discarded fries or the uneaten remains of somebody's Big Mac.

Rather than accept the terms of gleaning and the meager offerings she could hope to bring home for Naomi and herself, Ruth challenges the status quo and stretches the limits of the law. By the time Boaz arrives, she has already made a highly irregular request to the foreman that goes beyond his authority to grant. Until the landowner comes and she learns how the matter will turn out, she diligently sets to work, picking up bits of grain here and there without stopping for rest breaks.

Outrageous Ruth

In short order, Boaz's notices the new gleaner in his field and inquires of his foreman, "To whom does this young woman belong?" (Ruth 2:5, Hubbard translation). His question sounds like a line straight out of a Jane Austen novel—a pointed inquiry about a woman whose social standing is under scrutiny. "What are her connections?"

First impressions of Boaz are suddenly forgotten as we detect romantic interest in the mighty landowner. But wait a minute. This man is scrupulous. How can we reconcile the notion that a landowner of such impeccable character would think of scoping out the gleaners in his field in search of a prospective bride? Marriages were strategic opportunities for families to forge political and social ties with other families to strengthen their standing in the community. In this environment, for Boaz at least, Ruth was out of the running. Socially, a gleaner was lower than a field hand.[12] Boaz was in a different social league from Ruth.

Furthermore, this gleaner had a known history of barrenness, for her failure to deliver a son (or even a daughter for Mahlon) was no secret. Her qualifications would never match the search criteria of a man like Boaz. He would forfeit his standing as a man of valor if he shirked his family responsibilities by looking for a wife in the margins of society or choosing a woman who offered little hope of bearing a son.

The simplest explanation for why Boaz noticed her is that she was an unfamiliar face among the regular gleaners. Boaz isn't checking her social pedigree. His question is only intended to identify this stranger. A Hebrew scholar explains.

> In ancient Israelite society in general, the community to which one belonged—at all levels, family, clan, tribe, nation, village—- was central to one's identity and status.... In particular, a woman had no independent status and identity in Israel's patri- archal world. She belonged to and lived under the authority of her father when unmarried and her husband when married.[13]

Boaz soon discovers that the new gleaner is the young Moabi- tess who arrived with Naomi. A world of information is contained in this brief description, for all Bethlehem is talking about her. Now so are these two men—like the pitcher and the manager conferring in low tones on the baseball mound—occasionally glancing in Ruth's direction. Boaz is intrigued, for he has already heard the talk and is aware of the remarkable sacrifices Ruth has made to return with Naomi.

When the foreman explains Ruth's unusual request, no doubt Boaz's eyes widen. Traditionally, we've understood Ruth to be asking for permission to glean in Boaz's field. But this seems unlikely, since the law already permitted gleaners. Asking per- mission to glean was akin to asking a traffic cop for permission to walk on the public sidewalk. Ruth's subsequent display of gratitude appears excessive if not a bit ridiculous if Boaz is only consenting to what he already allows. Closer examination of this episode indicates Ruth is not being overly deferential nor is she playing coy games, as some think, to force a meeting with the wealthy master of the field. She is acting in character and boldly shaking things up once again. Ruth is asking to break the rules.

HOW BIG IS A CORNER?

Typically when harvesting a field, hired men went first—grasping handfuls of standing grain stalks with one hand, cutting them off at the base with a sickle, then laying the cut stalks on the ground. Female workers followed, gathering and binding cut grain into bundles to be carted to the threshing floor where raw kernels of grain were separated from the husks. Gleaners came last and were permitted in the field only *after* both teams of hired workers finished and bundled sheaves of grain were removed from the field.

Ruth requested that Boaz suspend this long-established practice for her. She didn't want to pick up leftover scraps for Naomi. She wanted to feed her mother-in-law. So she made a proposal to ensure that both she and Naomi would have enough to eat. She asked to "glean and gather among the sheaves *behind* the harvesters" (Ruth 2:7, emphasis added). In other words, Ruth asked to go where gleaners were not permitted, to work *among* the harvesters where plenty of newly cut grain lay waiting to be gathered into bundles. Robert Hubbard writes with admiration:

> Given the meager fare gleaners probably gathered, one suspects a concern to increase her chances of gleaning enough to provide for Naomi and herself.... Ruth showed herself to be anything but a modest, self-effacing foreigner. Rather, she emerges as courageous, if not slightly brash. Probably aware of possible rejection and ostracism, she willingly took a sizable risk in order to benefit her mother-in-law. Again, she lived out her well-articulated fidelity (1:16–17) and presented a model of risk-taking devotion to be emulated.[14]

The young Moabitess brings an outsider's perspective to practices the Israelites had been observing for generations. Like the child who in a clear voice innocently announces that the emperor has no clothes, Ruth's advocacy for Naomi exposes the shortcomings of God's people. Sometimes newcomers have a way of showing us we've settled into a narrow, precise obedience—a tidy conformity to the law—that falls far short of what God really intends.

Jesus was that kind of newcomer in his day, another outsider to the religious establishment. His teachings reveal that obedience to God is not a matter of precision (which was what the Pharisees thought), but that the parameters of true obedience are virtually limitless. We can't reduce life with God to a checklist of rules to be kept and deadly sins to be avoided. The Sermon on the Mount knocked down the walls that religious living had constructed around God's law and pointed to a way of living that goes beyond the letter of the law to the spirit. Formal religion only takes us so far—for it is both safe and doable. Love, however, knows no limits, takes costly risks, and looks for ways to give more.

Even though Ruth was only a beginner, she was learning in the ordinary, everyday moments of life what it means to be a daughter of Yahweh and the kind of bold living that loving God produces. Simply by doing what she knew to be right, Ruth's actions elevate the discussion of the law to a completely different realm.

Boaz gets the shock of his life when a first-time gleaner—a foreigner at that—takes him to a higher level of obedience. By her actions, Ruth is not merely going the distance to fight for her mother-in-law's needs, she is also pressing Boaz to color outside the lines of his understanding of God's law. The letter of the law says, "Let them glean." The spirit of the law says, "Feed them." Two entirely different concepts. Ruth's bold proposal exposes the difference.

God's law creates a healthy conflict of interest for Boaz. At harvesttime, God meant for landowners like Boaz to wrestle with such basic questions as, How big is a corner? How wide is an edge? How thoroughly do I want my workers to clear my fields of grain, given the fact that we only have one chance to clear it? How much will I leave behind for the poor? Walking with God takes us into a sea of possibilities that stretch our capacity for sacrifice and our imagination for obedience, reminding us there's always more to following God than we think.

A Blessed Alliance

All eyes are on Boaz, waiting for his reply. Will he brush her off or lash out over the forwardness of this foreigner? The Moabitess has gone too far. Ruth has crossed the line. Israelite protocol has been breeched. Will he eject her from his field? Will Boaz prove tightfisted, or will he open his hand?

Boaz's response is as astonishing as Ruth's request is outrageous, and this is where our strong admiration for Boaz begins to grow. Instead of becoming defensive (this is his field, after all, and he *is* the boss), the lights go on and he fully embraces her suggestion. Instead of being displeased or offended, he is moved to act on her behalf. Boaz's godliness is real, and he willingly follows Ruth's lead. He actually appears driven—you might even say obsessed—to come up with ways of making her mission possible. In an astonishing outpouring of grace, Boaz exceeds the young Moabitess' request.

What follows is an openhearted sequence of actions where Boaz extends his hand and his resources to ensure Ruth's success. Yes, by all means, she may glean among the reapers where there will be plenty of grain for her. He grants her special rights in his fields for the entire harvest season and urges her not to wander into other fields, but to glean only with his servant girls.

Boaz personally guarantees her safety. "I have told the men not to touch you" (Ruth 2:9)—protection she will need when venturing into restricted zones where gleaners are banned and harvesters might mistreat her. His words, while reassuring, also reflect the real dangers women faced even in a godly landowner's field. Boaz then invites Ruth to drink from the water jars his men fill. Now she won't forfeit precious gleaning time by going elsewhere in search of water to quench her thirst.

> Ruth is overwhelmed. She drops to her knees, then bows to the ground in an oriental gesture of gratitude. Here is the landowner whose favor she was seeking, and he is more generous than she could have hoped.[15]

Let us be clear. Boaz is not motivated by sudden infatuation, but by a heart for Yahweh and by his deep respect and admiration for Ruth's unprecedented kindness to Naomi. He knows she has given up much to come to Bethlehem with Naomi. And now with his own eyes, he sees her taking enormous risks as she gleans for the sake of her mother-in-law and giving Bethlehemites more to talk about. You can be sure this day's events were soon added to local dinner conversations about the young Moabitess.

Then, in words that soothed Ruth's aching heart, Boaz opens his heart in blessing, as he prays, "May the LORD repay you for what you have done. May you be richly rewarded by the LORD, the God of Israel, under whose wings you have come to take refuge" (Ruth 2:12). Boaz, of course, is unaware that he will, himself, have a hand in how God answers his prayer.

Until this moment, Ruth's interior world has been curtained off from us. The narrator hasn't disclosed the inner workings of her heart. There were earlier hints in the story of her grief, but here, in this exchange with Boaz, we catch a glimpse of evidence that she is sorrowing as deeply as Naomi. In response to Boaz's kindness and to his gentle words of blessing, Ruth responds, "You have given me *comfort* and have spoken kindly to your servant — though I do not have the standing of one of your servant girls" (Ruth 2:13, emphasis added).

THE PLUS FACTOR

Boaz isn't finished. He has more ideas and will literally fuel her efforts. At mealtime, he invites Ruth to join his table and share a meal with his workers. When she does, Boaz serves her himself, heaping more roasted grain for her than she can possibly eat.

Hubbard sees Boaz pulling Ruth into the circle of his household by making her the "most favored gleaner." He explains. "In modern terms, by giving access to the water cooler and the lunchroom, Boaz resembled a boss showing a new employee around the company."[16] Although Boaz wasn't hiring Ruth, his actions create a powerful gospel scene: a gleaner seated alongside paid workers, a Moabitess "dining" with Israelites, a man serving a woman, the poor included among the rich, an outsider embraced by the inner circle. Looks like the kind of feasting Jesus would have enjoyed, a prefiguring of the kind of world his gospel restores, where "there is neither Jew nor Greek, slave nor free, male nor female, for you are all one in Christ Jesus" (Galatians 3:28). Ruth was on the losing end of all three categories, but Boaz refuses to maintain those boundaries. Ruth embraced God's people sight unseen on the road from Moab. Now they are embracing her.

But the impact of their actions—both Ruth's and Boaz's—does not stop with this meal. Boaz issues directives to his workers. Now the pressure is on for *them* to act sacrificially. Boaz not only instructs them not to touch or harass her in any way, he wants the men deliberately to place stalks of cut grain in her path. Following Boaz's example, they are not simply to permit; they are to promote. He makes his workers responsible for making sure Ruth does not go home empty-handed.

FEMININE QUALITIES

Who would imagine that the simple task of providing food for a woman's family would shake up an entire community and move others to reach for a higher level of obedience? Ruth's story is good for us to contemplate when we crawl out of bed in the morning. Sometimes our days are filled with activities we love. Sometimes the battles before us aren't what we expected to be doing with our lives, much less what we expected to be doing as women. The backbreaking work Ruth did all day was hardly the feminine occupation she envisioned for herself. But she was doing God's work—perspiration, dirty and broken fingernails, rough surroundings, and all—and she did it with all of her might, her resources, and her wit. Ultimately, her bold initiatives bless God's people, challenging them to contemplate what it means to live as Yahweh's people, and Ruth herself becomes a powerful catalyst for change.

God gave us Ruth and Sojourner Truth to remind us that courage, boldness, and godly leadership are important feminine attributes when it comes to living for God. When we swim upstream against the culture; use our voices to speak the truth; advocate stubbornly for others; and sweat, toil, and strategize to advance God's kingdom on earth, we are doing woman's work. *And ain't I a woman?*

HOME ALONE

While Ruth works all day in the barley field, a very different scene is playing out back at the house. There Naomi sits in solitude — waiting and worrying. What a wretched day for her. "Is Ruth okay? Did she get lost? Is anyone mistreating her? How hungry and tired she must be." Without the convenience of cell phones, there won't be any periodic updates from Ruth. Naomi must wait until evening to hear how Ruth fared on her bold and dangerous venture. Had she suspected how far her daughter-in-law would go to achieve success, she would have had even greater cause for concern.

Every mother who has ever stayed up into the wee hours of the night, waiting for a teenager to come home after curfew, knows this routine. Anxiety and waiting have a way of slowing down the clock — stretching minutes into endlessness. Imagination and fear run wild. Naomi's ears prick up at the slightest sound of footsteps in the distance. She glances out the window and strains her eyes. How many times was it just a neighbor passing by her house? At last one set of trudging footsteps finally reach the door. It opens. Ruth is home.

DISCUSSION QUESTIONS

1. Describe a situation where you (or someone you know) faced adversity and had to do things to survive or make ends meet that you never imagined doing.

2. Compare Ruth's and Naomi's outlooks at the start of their new life in Bethlehem. Why did they see things so differently?

3. How did gleaning give the poor dignity? And how did it put them at risk?

4. What healthy "conflict of interest" did God's gleaning laws pose for the landowner and his workers? Why is this conflict important for us?

5. Why is it easier to live by the letter of the law than by the spirit?

6. What can we learn from Ruth's bold initiative?

7. Why was her courage important to Boaz?

8. Describe some areas of your life where you need to be bolder for God's kingdom.

Chapter Five

THE POWER OF *HESED*

"What's love got to do with it?"

Tina Turner's Grammy-winning hit shoots up a warning flare. The heart is in danger when love is involved. The potential for pain is alarming. Better to keep your guard up than risk being wounded by something so fickle and lethal as love. Love (once we let it in) has tremendous power over us. Some of our deepest scars come from injuries inflicted by those we loved or thought loved us. Turner's advice is to indulge in the pleasure without risking the pain that can come from letting your heart get involved. Having learned the hard way just how painfully traumatic a love gone bad can be, she is only being honest and self-protective when she questions somewhat defiantly, "Who needs a heart?"

Similar forebodings sometimes surface in the church. Just days before Frank and I married, an elderly lady in my church hobbled up and offered a Tina Turner warning to me. Wagging her finger in my face, she cautioned with the thin raspy voice of experience, "Marriage isn't all a bed of roses." She wanted to alert me that, like a shooting star, new love's early burst of passion can fizzle out quickly. The once all-consuming relationship coasts into dull disappointment, and the person you thought you couldn't live without turns out to be someone you wouldn't choose for a friend. Singles looking for that right person are sure it will never happen to them. Those whose marriages have gone cold remind us by their disinterested looks or by filing for divorce that it can.

While I don't take lightly what Tina Turner endured in her tumultuous marriage, I don't share her jaded philosophy of relationships or her misguided solution. Nor do I want to wag a pessimistic finger in the faces of prospective brides. Still, there's a good bit of truth to the notion that love comes with risks. Few sorrows in this world are capable of creating the terrible void left behind by a love that is lost—not just the love between a man and a woman, but of parent and child, brother and sister, or the deeply satisfying David-and-Jonathan love of a friend. When you're in the throes of heartache over a love lost by death, betrayal, estrangement, or simply dwindling interest, it's easy to buy into the notion that you're better off to barricade your heart against the hazards of love.

The Price of Love

If we happened upon Naomi's journal lying open to the entry made the morning after she and Ruth returned from Moab, we might find words like those written by St. Augustine in the aftermath of the death of Nebridius, a friend he described as "the half of my soul."[1]

> My heart was black with grief. Whatever I looked upon had the air of death. My native place was a prison-house and my home a strange unhappiness. The things we had done together became sheer torment without him. My eyes were restless looking for him, but he was not there. I hated all places because he was not in them.[2]

Bad as things were for Naomi in Moab, coming back to Bethlehem probably made things even worse. This was where she and Elimelech shared so many joys and dreams and where their terrible nightmare started. Like the untouched closet—that sacred shrine where a lost loved one's clothing still hang and scents of him still linger—Bethlehem held countless reminders of Elimelech, of the past, and of their boys that stirred up tender memories and blanketed Naomi with a dark cloud of depression. Naomi surely wondered, as countless mourners do, if she'd ever come out from under the fog. Love had everything to do with Naomi's sufferings—the love that lay buried in three simple graves back in Moab, and the greater love lost somewhere back in Moab (maybe even before) when God stopped loving her. That's what she believed, and her heart, like Augustine's, was black with grief.

When things go wrong in our lives, we don't usually pull out our moral calculator and begin tallying up all the black marks on our record to figure out if we deserve what's happening to us. Naomi doesn't do that either.[3] She just speaks honestly about how things look from where she sits. Judging from the evidence, the God she once thought loved her, doesn't. This makes no sense to her. She isn't a pagan idolater. She's a believing Israelite—one of God's chosen people, a faithful follower of Yahweh. Yet the God she trusted with her heart, the Almighty One she counted on to be there for her, has turned against her. Instead of loving her, he has become her enemy, and she hasn't a clue why. Katharine Doob Sakenfeld sympathetically probes Naomi's despair.

> [Naomi] can see no reason and sees no way out.... She is physically alive, but from an emotional and psychological point of view, she views her life as already over.... Readers of this story who have grieved deeply themselves or who have accompanied a close friend or relative on that path will more easily grasp the way in which this entire book may be read as a story about Naomi as much as one about Ruth.... It is her loss and her despair that must be addressed in what follows.[4]

How do God's love and so much pain fit into the same picture? For Naomi, they don't. And so, because she cannot rid herself of the pain, she throws out God's love. Naomi pitches her tent in this dark place. That's where she is camping the morning Ruth sets out to glean. So when Ruth steps inside the door that evening, Naomi is completely unprepared for what happens next.

RUTH BRINGS HOME THE BACON

I can picture Ruth as she bundles the pile of winnowed grain in her shawl, slings it over her shoulder, and makes her way back to Bethlehem. After a long, hard day of backbreaking work in the hot sun, she has to feel exhausted. At the same time, the anticipation of Naomi's reaction surely brings a smile to Ruth's face and a much-needed spurt of energy as she trudges home that evening.

The quantity of raw grain that an average gleaner brought home from a day's work is anyone's guess—hopefully enough to get by for another day. But the amount Ruth lugs home belongs in the *Guinness Book of Records*. After gleaning and winnowing, she has accumulated an *ephah* of barley. Scholars estimate Ruth has brought home approximately *twenty-nine pounds* of grain. "Such a startling quantity of grain testified both to Boaz's generosity and Ruth's industry,"[5] not to mention the remarkable openhandedness of Boaz's workers. To put Ruth's gleanings in perspective, Old Babylonian records from that era indicate that a male worker's take-home pay for a day's labor was rarely more than one or two pounds. So in a single day Ruth's take was the rough equivalent of a half-month's wages or more. She raked in a minimum of *fifteen* times what Boaz's harvesters were pocketing as a fair day's wage.[6]

If someone had alerted Naomi that Ruth was coming home with such a load, she never would have believed them. The emotional whiplash that Ruth's gleanings caused Naomi was akin to having the dreaded government car pull up in front of your house with military officers coming to break the news—not that your soldier son is a casualty of war, but that he is being decorated for heroism. The oversized load of raw grain was only the first surprise.

Next, Ruth reached inside her cloak and drew out the leftovers from her lunch—further evidence of her tender care for Naomi. How long had it been since the older widow had eaten?

It would take at least an hour or two to grind the raw barley, prepare the dough, and bake the bread. Even that would have been a welcome prospect for a hungry Naomi. Now there was no need to wait. Here was a ready-to-eat meal of roasted grain—the first fast-food dinner in the Bible. Dr. Hubbard enters into the moment. "By now Naomi's head was probably spinning. To glean so much grain was astounding, but to come home with cooked food was a shock that required explaining."[7]

NAOMI REVIVES

Naomi's questions come in a rush. Even before Ruth has a chance to answer, Naomi blesses her unknown benefactor. "Where did you glean today? Where did you work? Blessed be the man who took notice of you!" (Ruth 2:19). The answer to these questions will, of course, astonish Naomi again, for now she learns from Ruth what we have known all along. Her daughter-in-law has been working in a field that belongs to one of her husband's relatives. As if to drag out the suspense as long as possible, the narrator tacks the generous landowner's name at the far end of Ruth's sentence. "The name of the man I worked with today is Boaz" (2:19).

This news triggers an immediate and dramatic transformation in Naomi that I frankly find a little hard to believe. Lips that were formerly bitter with lament now overflow with blessing. The depression that has been holding Naomi hostage seems suddenly to release its grip. In a blink, Mara and her bitterness depart. Pleasant Naomi is back, this time with an appeal for Yahweh to pour out blessings on Boaz (Ruth 2:20): "The LORD bless him!" she exclaims with unexpected warmth. "*He* has not stopped showing his kindness [*hesed*] to the living and the dead" (2:20, emphasis added). What could possibly explain such an extravagant outpouring of generosity? What moved Boaz to show such favor, prompting him even to exceed Ruth's original request? And how could something so ordinary as a load of barley and a dinner of roasted grain possess the power to pull Naomi out of her despondency?

As the standard explanation goes, Boaz was captivated from the first moment he saw Ruth, and his romantic interest sparked his generosity. But I find this reasoning problematic, since it implies that Boaz had ulterior motives in being kind, which hardly fits a man of his high reputation. Naomi supposedly perks up when she catches wind of a budding romance between Ruth and Boaz and sees a new role for herself as matchmaker in bringing the pair together.

At this point, romance begins to dominate our thinking. We are only too happy to drop the unfinished business of Naomi's earlier complaints against God. We assume Naomi drops them too. Besides, after so much angst, we're ready to move on to pleasanter subjects—flip through the current issue of *Brides Magazine*, phone the caterer, and reserve the wedding chapel. Most of us have bought into this fairy-tale rendition of Ruth's story. I plead guilty for holding this view myself in the past. Now, however, I'm finding these explanations unsatisfactory.

The secret to unraveling these mysteries is one and the same. The motive of Boaz's lavish generosity toward the two widows and the cause of Naomi's miraculous transformation—indeed the choices and actions in the entire book of Ruth—are bound up in the simple but utterly rich Hebrew word *hesed*.

LOST IN TRANSLATION

I once heard the story of a Bible translator who, when stumped by how best to translate the word "lamb" for a people who had never seen a lamb, decided to substitute the word "llama"—a familiar animal in that region. In a way, the choice made sense. Both animals have four legs, are woolly, and eat grass. But unlike sheep, llamas are known to be crotchety and sometimes aggressive in disposition, prone to spitting and even neck wrestling when threatened. They're much larger too. A llama isn't anything like the silent, defenseless little lamb, and misses the point completely.

Translators face a similar dilemma when they come across the Hebrew word *hesed* in the ancient Old Testament text, for no word in the English language captures its exact meaning. Consequently, they end up settling for llamas, and we end up with a smorgasbord of words like "kindness," "mercy," "loyalty," "loving-kindness," "loyal, steadfast, unfailing (or just plain) love"—words that certainly touch on what *hesed* means but by themselves don't begin to do justice to this powerful, richly laden word. As a result, we easily skim over references to *hesed* without realizing we have just stumbled over one of the most potent words in the Old Testament.

With a little help from Hebrew scholars, we can come a little closer to the meaning of *hesed* than a llama is to a lamb. They tell us *hesed* is a strong Hebrew word that sums up the ideal lifestyle for God's people. It's the way God intended for human beings to live together from the beginning—the "love-your-neighbor-as-yourself" brand of living, an active, selfless, sacrificial caring for one another that goes against the grain of our fallen natures.

Two parties are involved—someone in desperate need and a second person who possesses the power and the resources to make a difference.[8] *Hesed* is driven, not by duty or legal obligation, but by a bone-deep commitment—a loyal, selfless love that motivates a person to do voluntarily what no one has a right to expect or ask of them. They have the freedom to act or to walk away without the slightest injury to their reputation. Yet they willingly pour themselves out for the good of someone else. It's actually the kind of love we find most fully expressed in Jesus. In a nutshell, *hesed* is the gospel lived out.

Hesed in Action

The narrator of the Ruth story doesn't bog down with definitions to help us understand what *hesed* is all about. Instead, he provides colorful pictures to show us how *hesed* looks in people's lives. Actually, this photo album approach is especially fitting because *hesed* is something you do[9] more than something you think or feel or a mood created by candlelight dinners and violins. It's hard to grasp the power of it until you see it in action. Besides, most of us do better with pictures anyway.

Although the word *hesed* appears only three times in the narrative, the book of Ruth is thoroughly soaked in it. Naomi is first to bring it up when she blesses her Moabite daughters-in-law and attempts to send them away. "May the LORD show kindness to you [lit., 'do with you *hesed*'], as you have shown to your dead and to me" (Ruth 1:8b). This is not just a polite farewell. Naomi's parting wish for her daughters-in-law is that they would be on the receiving end of Yahweh's *hesed*.

To illustrate what she means by *hesed*, Naomi points to Orpah's and Ruth's devoted and selfless behavior toward their husbands and Naomi herself in Moab when things were falling apart—high praise coming from Naomi that reflects the extraordinary character of her daughters-in-law. Ironically, in the act of emancipating her daughters-in-law, Naomi is herself displaying *hesed*, for she is voluntarily putting their interests, their futures, their happiness ahead of her own desperate need for assistance and companionship. Hers is the first great loving sacrifice in the book.

When Naomi sees Ruth's load of grain, she brings up *hesed* again. Such extraordinary generosity could only have one explanation. *Hesed* is at work. "He has not stopped showing his kindness [*hesed*] to the living and the dead" (Ruth 2:20). According to Naomi, *hesed* (and not infatuation with Ruth) is the true motive behind this outpouring of favor toward Ruth and herself.

When Ruth approaches Boaz at the threshing floor, *hesed* surfaces yet again. This time Boaz is the one to name it. "The LORD bless you, my daughter.... *This* kindness [*hesed*] is greater than that which you showed earlier" (Ruth 3:10, emphasis added). In the eyes of Boaz, Ruth did *hesed* to Naomi when she relinquished her freedom and bound herself to Naomi for life. She did *hesed* again when she boldly pressed for greater gleaning privileges in the barley field. But, in Boaz's eyes, those powerful displays of *hesed* pale in comparison to what Ruth will do for Naomi before the story ends.

So while there's still a lot about *hesed* that we don't yet fully understand, we can at least begin to sketch the outlines of what *hesed* is all about from these examples. According to what we have seen, *hesed* can be boiled down to this: *Someone cares and has freely made it their business to look out for you.* To make sure we get the message, the narrator spotlights individuals whose actions are ordinary and expected, but fall short of *hesed*. Orpah, for example, serves this purpose in the first part of the story. She makes a sensible choice that in the culture was viewed as entirely acceptable. Ruth, however, does *hesed* for Naomi—the extraordinary, the unexpected, and the exceptional. Her choice is radical and costly, but she acts in complete freedom.

THE TROUBLE WITH *HESED*

Hesed lies at the heart of the high points of Naomi's story. But *hesed* is also the crux of her lows. Naomi grew up in a world that was built on Yahweh's *hesed* for his people. This was the bedrock of the nation's faith and hope, the glue that held together the history of her people and the promise of their future. God had pledged himself to them. They were his people. He was their God. They drew confidence and hope from the fact that Yahweh was "abounding in love [*hesed*]" (Exodus 34:6).

Yet instead of sensing the warmth of his care, the shelter of his wing, or the steadfastness of his *hesed*, Naomi was exposed to the elements. Here, in the wake of one tragedy after another, the thought of God's *hesed* appears confusing and more of a contradiction than a comfort to the weather-beaten Naomi. The magnitude of her distress becomes clearer when we realize that we were created to live in God's *hesed*—to dwell in his love and to thrive on his care. Having God's *hesed* is the best thing that could ever happen to anyone. And nothing in this world is worse than living without it. So Naomi isn't simply grieving the fact that her life has fallen to pieces. Nor is she doubting God's existence. She is lamenting the fact that she has lost Yahweh's *hesed*, and in this she has suffered the ultimate loss. In light of this, the emptiness she bewails takes on a whole new meaning.

God's *hesed* is the centerpiece of the Ruth story, as it should be. The entire book zeros in on the weighty question of whether God's *hesed* has run out for Naomi. It's a question that sooner or later all of us will have to face for ourselves or for someone we love. And the story addresses this question, not by a spectacular vision or a divine voice speaking out of the heavens, but by God's people engaged in simple yet extraordinary acts of *hesed*.

NAOMI — UP CLOSE AND PERSONAL

Given the choice, I much prefer to look at Naomi from afar, give her the voice she has been denied for too long, and deal gently and sympathetically with her crisis of soul. Right in the middle of writing this chapter, that choice was taken away from me. Instead of observing and analyzing Naomi from a comfortable distance, I found myself sitting next to her in the darkness and the pain, wondering what had happened to God's *hesed* for me. A dark cloud settled over me, and my study of *hesed* took on a personal dimension I didn't expect or want. I wouldn't write another word for weeks.

It all started late one night when, as I was sitting at my computer thinking and writing about *hesed*, the phone rang. It was my mother-in-law, and I could tell right away from the frightened tone of her voice that something was terribly wrong. My husband's brother, Kelly — an experienced mountain climber — was in desperate trouble somewhere near the summit of Mt. Hood in Oregon. He had managed to connect briefly by cell phone (with his wife Karen and his sons) to signal an SOS and give scant details. He was in a snow cave, and his two climbing buddies, Brian Hall and Jerry "Nikko" Cooke, had left him there to go for help.

The little information we had was enough for Frank to board a plane for Portland the next day. Both of us were worried sick. The following morning, Frank was on the mountain, and I was waiting anxiously for word of what was happening. I turned on the television to see if CNN had picked up the story and was startled to see my husband's face on the screen. What started out as a private family crisis quickly escalated into a national media event. For more than a week, the story captivated the media, and across the country people were glued to their televisions, tracking developments that would end in a triple tragedy.

All those events seem like a blur to me now. The crisis was desperate with three men lost on the mountain. Unprecedented levels of resources, technology, and volunteers poured in from all directions. Search and rescue experts dropped what they were doing, strapped on their gear, and headed for the mountain—ready to do whatever it took to bring the missing climbers safely home. Family members boldly spoke words of faith on network television. "Courage and hope"—how we clung to those words. God's people everywhere mobilized to pray. And believe it or not, mockers were on the Internet, ridiculing our faith in God. Media cameras zoomed in, and all America waited and watched. If ever there was a moment for the perfect miracle, this was it.

Yet, to our utter dismay, the skies didn't clear and the storms didn't stop. Instead of a miracle, blizzards barreled in with record fury, driving rescue workers off the mountain for the most critical days of the search. By the time the skies did clear and rescue workers located Kelly's snow cave, it was too late. Our hearts sank again when the search effort for Brian and Nikko was downshifted from "rescue" to "recovery."

Nothing could have prepared us for the avalanche of grief that descended on the James family. Words I wrote earlier in this book had become a terrible reality. For my sister-in-law, Karen, widowhood had arrived live on CNN. Like Naomi, my mother-in-law was stricken with the loss of a son. And my husband, who had spoken courageously for all of us before a watching world, was devastated by the loss of his beloved brother.

In the aftermath of loss and grief, Naomi's questions came to me as I struggled to put God's *hesed* for our family alongside such a tragic outcome. Then I asked myself who I would rather hear from in my struggle with God? Someone whose life is picture-perfect and doesn't have a scratch? Or a broken-down Naomi whose views of *hesed* have withstood the multiple assaults of grief and loss, isolation and poverty, depression and despair? In my own struggle, I found my interest deepening in what Naomi will conclude.

HESED GETS THROUGH

In a way, the grain Ruth spread at Naomi's feet that night and the meal that filled her empty stomach were like a pair of gloves Frank brought back from the mountain. Coming from Florida, he wasn't exactly winterized for the chilling temperatures on Mt. Hood. Late one night in the early stages of the crisis, Frank was giving a series of network interviews outdoors in the bitter cold mountain air. He was wearing Kelly's red jacket, but Frank's bare hands were freezing. A CNN producer noticed and offered his gloves to Frank. When the interviews were over, the producer refused to take his gloves back. In the midst of what was for Frank a life-altering tragedy, a pair of gloves seems hardly worth mentioning. But for some strange reason, he often refers to that simple act of kindness (dare we call it *hesed*?) as a moment that touched him deeply.

If someone gives you a pair of gloves when the sun is shining and your hands are warm, it doesn't mean that much. If you're well-fed and have plenty of food in your cupboard, a sack of grain and a ready-to-eat meal seem ordinary and perhaps a little boring. Prosperity tends to dull our senses to the presence of God's *hesed* in our lives. But, when trouble strikes and you're sitting in the darkness with a heart that aches for him, the slightest sign of his presence is monumental. A load of grain, a cooked meal, or a pair of gloves sends a signal—faint though it may be—that he is here and he hasn't forgotten. Naomi's experience is a lot like watching a heart monitor gone flat and suddenly seeing the flicker of a pulse. It is an exhilarating moment—the best possible news for the despairing Naomi, for now she knows God's *hesed* is still here and it is meant for her.

Not only does Naomi realize through the actions of Boaz that God is still doing *hesed* for her, she makes the stunning discovery that *hesed* is still actively at work for Elimelech, Mahlon, and Kilion—"the living *and the dead*" (Ruth 2:20, emphasis added).

Boaz's great act of kindness for his relatives' family signals that Elimelech and his sons are not forgotten either.

Ruth's *hesed* for Naomi contains that kind of longevity too, for it will not expire at Naomi's graveside or if a better opportunity surfaces for Ruth. "Where you die, I will die — there will I be buried. May the LORD do thus and so to me, and more as well, *if even death* parts me from you!" (Ruth 1:17, NRSV, emphasis added). Which means that, somewhere in the vicinity of Bethlehem, a single grave contains the bones of two women — Naomi and her daughter-in-law Ruth. Even in death, Ruth is still doing *hesed*. Naomi is not alone. This is the Gospel of Ruth.

HESED AND THE MILKMAN

God's unending supply of *hesed* for his people reminds me of a practice from a bygone era that is still in force overseas. Every morning in Oxford, when it was still dark and residents of our student flats were still in bed, we could hear the milkman making his rounds — small milk bottles clinking in his wire carrier, the sound of footsteps as he bolted up the steps — leaving two or three fresh bottles of milk by every door.

According to the prophet Jeremiah who, like Naomi, had reason to believe God's *hesed* had run out, God delivers a fresh supply every morning. "Yet this I call to mind and therefore I have hope: Because of the LORD's great love [*hesed*] we are not consumed, for his compassions never fail. They are new every morning; great is your faithfulness" (Lamentations 3:21 – 23).

This is the world of Naomi — a world where trouble and God's *hesed* sit side by side. She goes to sleep that night with a full stomach, enough grain on hand to last for days, and her head resting on the pillow of God's *hesed*. The famine is over. Hunger has been banished at last. Ruth and Boaz will see to that. To top it off, Boaz has extended special gleaning privileges to Ruth for the duration of the harvest season, instructing her to continue working in his fields with his maids. You can almost feel the weight of worry rolling off of Naomi. Ruth's safety is secure, for Boaz has lowered a protective shield around the Moabitess. Anyone who touches her will be dealing with this man of valor. Hard to believe a day that commenced with such dreary prospects could contain so much goodness.

But Naomi's troubles aren't over. The pillow next to hers is still empty. She will still shed plenty of tears. She remains in poverty, in the margins of society, and Ruth will still go out to glean. So how do we piece this all together? Seems like we've ended up where we started—with God's love and a lot of pain together in the same picture.

What Naomi teaches us (and what we need to cling to as tenaciously as she is learning to do) is the fact that God's *hesed* is non-negotiable. When trouble invaded Naomi's life, she was mistaken to throw out God's love. God *never* stops loving his child. But we are equally mistaken to throw out sorrow when something good happens to her. Loss and grief are permanent fixtures in Naomi's life. The intensity of her pain will subside, but her broken heart will never be completely whole. That is the high price of loving. That is reality in our broken world.

According to Naomi's story, *both* pain and love are present in this life, and the one does not eliminate the other. Good and bad. God's *hesed* and heartache. Together. In the same picture. So when trouble strikes—whether in a late-night phone call, a mountain blizzard that doesn't let up, heartbreaks from the past, or fears for tomorrow—the one thing we can be certain of is that God's love for us is still actively in force. To answer Tina Turner, a deeper *hesed* brand of love has everything to do with what is happening to us. Living by faith means hanging on to God's *hesed* and trusting him, even when we're looking at him from ground zero.

After the passing of Elimelech, Mahlon, and Kilion, there are no more deaths in the book of Ruth. But before the story is over, lives will be laid down, even greater sacrifices will be made, and more lavish *hesed* offered for Naomi's good, for the dimensions of *hesed* know no limits. Even Naomi herself will be caught up in the action, not simply as a recipient of *hesed*, but also as a giver.

But before we move on to the next episode in the story of Naomi, Ruth, and Boaz, we need to take up one more matter—-

another vital issue that this story raises for us. We've been reassured of God's love, even when trouble is overwhelming us. But how is God acting on his love? If we were to dust our own lives for his fingerprints, what would we discover?

DISCUSSION QUESTIONS

1. Describe a time in your life when you had reason to doubt God's love for you.

2. Why does Naomi doubt God's love?

3. What is *hesed* and how does it picture Jesus' gospel?

4. How and why does Ruth do *hesed* to Naomi, and why do love and selflessness describe her actions?

5. What causes Boaz to join Ruth's cause, and what does this tell us about the kind of man he was?

6. Why does Naomi revive when Ruth returns with surprising news?

7. Why is it sometimes difficult for Naomi and for you to believe God is overflowing in *hesed*?

8. How does Jesus reassure you of God's love, even when your life is full of trouble?

Chapter Six

FINDING GOD'S FINGERPRINTS ON OUR LIVES

"It was a God-thing."

This late twentieth-century catchphrase has managed to survive (at least for a few years) into the twenty-first century as a handy way to describe something wonderful and unexpected that happens—something we can't explain to ourselves in terms of human activity or natural cause and effect. We were miraculously spared from a terrible accident. We got the dream job. The chemo worked. We bumped into an old friend, just as we were thinking of them. Some odd-shaped piece of our lives clicked neatly into place. "It was a God-thing."

Although this phrase never appears in the book of Ruth, nearly every reader spots the Old Testament equivalent when they come across the statement that puts Ruth on a collision course with Boaz. "*As it turned out*, she found herself working in a field belonging to Boaz" (Ruth 2:3, emphasis added). Ruth's choice of a barley field, while completely random to her, was certainly no accident as subsequent events reveal. God nudged her in the direction of the field belonging to Boaz, and now both Ruth's and Naomi's fortunes take a definite upturn. Like crime scene investigators, readers dusting for evidence of God's involvement in the story are elated to uncover a perfect set of his fingerprints.

This singling out of specific fortuitous events as places where, from our perspective, God seems to be actively orchestrating things is deeply heartening at one level. We desperately want him to be active in our lives and mostly think of his involvement in ways that turn out well for us. So we're profoundly encouraged when we see it. Yet, at another level, such thinking can also lead us down the wrong path.

We can end up with a view of God that is more like a fairy godmother—showing up from time to time to wave a sparkling wand and bring a little magic into our lives. Or like a superhero waiting in the wings for just the right moment to step in and rescue us from disaster. A view like this doesn't begin to come to terms with how complex, mysterious, and completely unpredictable God actually is or with his overarching agenda for our broken world or for our individual lives.

There is, of course, a certain benefit in limiting God's involvement in our lives to these occasional sightings. This way we can keep God at a comfortable distance from the awful things that happen to us and the tragedies we hear about in the daily news. If God only makes positive appearances, then we're spared from having to deal with awkward questions about why bad things happen under his watch. Yet, while I certainly don't want to take anything away from the notion that there are pleasant places in life when God's hand is evident (I rejoice in them myself), at the same time, it's scary to think God is somehow absent at crucial moments and from crises when we need him most.

Most of us experience, at some point during our lives, the kind of confusion Naomi suffered when we can't see a speck of evidence that God is present or working on our behalf. I must confess that in the aftermath of my brother-in-law Kelly's death, Naomi's questions about God carry new meaning for me. We're all in big trouble if we let go of the possibility that there is considerably more to God's involvement in our lives than what our senses are able to detect.

THE VIEW FROM OUTER SPACE

In the sixties, when the Americans and the Russians were competing in the space race, two conflicting views of God were transmitted from space capsules to earth. The first was attributed to Yuri Gagarin, a Russian cosmonaut and the first human being in space, who reported back from his 1961 foray beyond earth's orbit, "I don't see any God up here." In 1968 the American crew on the first manned mission to the moon radioed a different message—not that they had seen God, but that they were seeing evidence of his handiwork. A spellbound world listened while from lunar orbit the three Apollo 8 astronauts took turns reading from Genesis. "In the beginning God created the heavens and the earth...." According to these two polarized views, either we are alone in the universe and no one is looking out for us *or* there is a God who created this earth and who cares deeply about what goes on down here.

In the book of Ruth we are looking at the world and at God from Naomi's earthbound point of view. And while Naomi didn't have the benefit of space age technology to transmit her views of God to a listening public, her theology is no secret to the careful reader. She represents the historic beliefs of God's people, teachings she was steeped in from early childhood. As her story unfolds, beliefs about Yahweh she heard and embraced as a young Israelite girl feel the heat of searing life experiences, and issues centering on how God runs this world come to the forefront in Naomi's sufferings.

God's people lived with the assumption that God's hand is behind everything. Naomi grew up believing in Yahweh as the planning, initiating, proactive God who called Abraham out of Ur of the Chaldeans and forged a covenant with him and his descendants. He was the God who handpicked and groomed Moses to emancipate the Israelites from slavery in Egypt. Yahweh parted the Red Sea, sustained the nation for forty years of wilderness wanderings, and delivered fortified cities like Jericho into their hands. With a history like that, Naomi doesn't doubt who is running things down here. But her faith in Yahweh's *hesed* is shaken and her long-held convictions about his care are challenged when personal disaster strikes again and again and again.

Naomi's thinking takes us in an uncomfortable direction. She upsets our tidy views of God because her own views of his involvement (not just in world affairs, but in her personal affairs) are considerably messier and certainly cover a whole lot more of life than isolated sunny moments here and there.

What in the World Is God Doing?

Providence is the theological label the church has historically attached to the subject of how God governs this world. It is also a major theme developed in the book of Ruth. We are reading about a slice of ordinary life—real people in real relationships, facing real troubles, making difficult choices and costly sacrifices. Providence tells us there's a lot more going on than what we can see, for God is at work behind the scenes to keep things moving in the direction of his ultimate goal for us as individuals and also for this world.

Professional theologians describe providence as the way God sustains, cares for, and governs the world *so that* it moves toward the destiny he defined at creation. The late professor Stan Grenz explains. "According to the Bible, God does not set the wheels of the universe in motion and then abandon it to run on its own. Instead, he enters into relationship with what he makes ... providence focuses on God's activity in guiding the historical process with the goal of bringing to pass his intention for the world he creates."[1]

At creation, God cast his grand vision for planet Earth. It was an ambitious vision that included both *a people* and *a kingdom*. The people he envisioned would be like him—*male and female* in his image and likeness—reflecting his character and ways. His image bearers would speak and act and govern for him on earth. This grand partnership with the men and women he created is foundational to how he means to bring about the kingdom aspect of his vision.

Amazingly, God's idea of a partnership places enormous responsibility on his image bearers and also means he wants us to participate in what he is doing here on earth and intends for us to do so, not as isolated individuals, but *together*. Mirroring the unity and diversity of the Holy Trinity, men and women who join forces in this divinely Blessed Alliance rely on each other and work together as one body to spread his kingdom on this planet.

DUSTING THE BOOK OF RUTH

Historically, Christians have differed sharply over how they believe God's providence works. At one end are those who believe God has chosen to operate in response mode—waiting to see what we will do first and then responding accordingly. At the opposite end are those who believe God plans and orchestrates everything in minute detail. Sixteenth-century Swiss reformer Ulrich Zwingli described God's providence as so comprehensive as to encompass activities of "bugs, lice, and fleas ... worms, flies, gadflies, roaches [and] spiders." According to Zwingli, "Not even such a trifling thing as a dream makes its appearance without providence."[2]

I have no idea what Naomi thought about bugs or earthworms. This polarized debate is noticeably absent from her story. What we do learn from examining her words is that her view of God's providence was both down-to-earth and expansive enough to include everything that was happening to her. Looking back, Naomi would almost certainly agree that Ruth's momentous entry into the field of Boaz was "a God-thing"—an unexpected, miraculous turning point in the lives of all three individuals. But she clearly believed God's hand was behind other things as well.

Dusting the book itself for traces of God, there's actually little hard evidence that surfaces. No voice from heaven. No vision or prophetic voice. No thunderbolt moment or spectacular miracle. Just ordinary people living ordinary lives, dealing with problems, making decisions, getting married, raising families, putting food on the table, conducting business, and coping with grief. Really, it's all pretty normal. Early on, the author mentions that God intervenes and stops the famine (Ruth 1:6) and later on that he enables Ruth to conceive (4:13). Other than that, the activity we see is entirely carried out by humans.

Interestingly enough, the most frequent references to God in the whole book are found in the prayers of God's people. You will find prayers in every chapter. They ask God to be present, to bless, to guide, to reward, to prosper with family and with fame. These prayers underscore their conviction that God is paying attention, that he notices their acts of kindness, that what they do matters to him, and that he has it in his power to act or, as in Naomi's case, to allow suffering to come.

We may not find as many explicit references to what God is doing as we would like, but the text clearly assumes that God's people live under Yahweh's gaze. They believe he cares about them personally and is actively involved in every aspect of their lives — relationships, choices, activities, ups and downs.[3] He is, as Boaz believes, the wing of shelter and protection that is overshadowing Ruth the Moabitess (Ruth 2:12). Someone *is* watching over her.

PROVIDENCE AND SUFFERING

Naomi embraces this robust and comprehensive view of God's providence and doesn't let it go, even when nothing remains of her former life with Elimelech. What complicates Naomi's viewpoint and makes it disturbing at the same time is that while she clearly detects God's fingerprints on the bright side of life, she doesn't exempt him from involvement in the darker stretches of her journey. She found God's fingerprints all over the Moab chapter of her story. And that belief lay at the heart of what was bothering her. Why did an all-powerful, good God allow her suffering?

If God's fingerprints are all over our lives too and his *hesed* is as relentless for us as it was for Naomi, then what are we to think when things go wrong for us? The tragic accident happens. We lose our job. The cancer spreads. We bump into someone hurtful we've been trying to avoid. The broken pieces of our lives stay broken. What am I supposed to think when the blizzards whip up and Kelly freezes to death because search and rescue workers can't get to him? Putting *hesed* and providence together with shattering circumstances like these leaves us wondering all over again, What is God doing?

This is when it would be nice to board a spacecraft and look at our own lives from above earth's atmosphere—to be able to see the end from the beginning and how all the smaller pieces of our stories fit into the bigger story God is weaving. From the ground, about all we can see is where we happen to be at the moment—the pain and regrets, the losses, the broken-down lives. From the human vantage point, we only see bits and pieces of what he is doing, and sometimes we, like Naomi, can't see anything that helps us make sense of what is going wrong in our lives.

If Naomi had the benefit of heaven's perspective on what was happening in her life, she would see that the painful path she was traveling was not a dead end. What appears from Naomi's point of view to be a very private grief and a deeply personal struggle with God is actually a crucial piece of a larger master plan. Those who already know how her story turns out have seen that God is giving Naomi a key role in events that ultimately lead to the birth of Israel's mighty King David, and beyond that to the birth of Jesus—the clearest, strongest evidence that God cares more than anyone imagines about what happens to us here on earth. Earthbound Naomi would never know how big a role God was giving her. She doesn't even realize yet that God is using suffering to equip her for the pivotal role of raising a child who just happens to be the grandfather of Israel's future king.

And what will she teach this young child? Obed will hear lessons of *hesed*—lessons learned in the blackout days of her despair. Bedtime stories of family history and of her own confusing walk with God will lodge in young Obed's heart. He will pass Naomi's teachings on to his son Jesse, who will one day father a son named David who will absorb her wisdom too. And long after Naomi is gone, the Bethlehem hillside will echo with the music of a young shepherd-poet as he worships Yahweh for his *hesed*. "Surely your goodness and unfailing love [*hesed*] will pursue me all the days of my life" (Psalm 23:6, NLT)—truth passed down from one generation to the next that the future king will rely on in days to come.

Suffering doesn't interfere with God's purposes for Naomi. Instead, he employs her pain and confusion to deepen her relationship with him and to fortify her for the next chapter of her life. God harnesses the sufferings of his children and compels the bad things that happen to us to serve his good purposes for us and for our mission in this world. This doesn't fit with how we normally look at things, but author Eugene Peterson confirms that once again we've gotten things backwards, for this is how God has always worked with his own:

> We live in a time when everyone's goal is to be perpetually healthy and constantly happy.... If any one of us fails to live up to the standards that are advertised as normative, we are labeled as a problem to be solved, and a host of well-intentioned people rush to try out various cures on us.... The gospel offers a different view of suffering: in suffering we enter *the depths*; we are at the heart of things; we are near to where Christ was on the cross.[4]

I have to ask myself how I can possibly expect to know Jesus as he would want to be known if my life remains unscathed by trouble and grief. How can I hope to grasp anything of God's heart for this broken planet if I never weep because its brokenness touches me and breaks my heart? How can I reflect his image if I never share in his sufferings? And how will any of us ever learn to treasure his *hesed* and grace if we never experience phases where these blessings seem absent? I wish I could learn these lessons vicariously, but I'm afraid that isn't the norm for any of us. Without knowing suffering and confusion firsthand, we're stuck in the superficial and we cannot know, much less express, the heart of Christ for others.

Does Naomi see all of this? I don't think so. In the midst of the struggle, she is no different from us. She only feels the pain of loss and the misery of believing God has turned his back on her. But she will learn things about God in this dark place that she never would have noticed in the light. And through this painfully honest journey, God is building a history with his daughter that will fortify her confidence in him and make her wise for the task ahead. Rick Warren could have been thinking of Naomi when he wrote that "your most effective ministry will come out of your deepest hurts."[5]

A PROVIDENTIAL PITFALL

I remember being dumbfounded when a friend admitted he never prayed for his unbelieving father. "If God plans to save my dad, he will," he explained. "Praying won't make a difference. I trust God's providence." What sounded pious and godly on the surface is actually a terrible misunderstanding of what providence is all about. And yet, often those who affirm God's providence sink into a sort of passive, sometimes almost fatalistic, mode where we are "waiting on God to act."

This contradicts one of the central tenets of providence—*concurrence*—which is the fact that the "God in whom we confess faith invites us to participate with him in the completion of his program for the world."[6] His preferred method of getting things done is to work through his image bearers. We aren't spectators to what God is doing in the world, but *participants*. Right from the beginning and still today, he is fulfilling his great plan for the world through *our* actions and efforts. It may come as a surprise to some, but providence is one of the strongest incentives God could give us for bold, vigorous activism.

How this plays out in the book of Ruth is truly fascinating, for if you can say anything about the people in this book, it is that they are a people who pray. Prayer is woven into their conversations, and they seem almost instinctively to end their sentences by appealing for God to come to their aid. But they don't stop with prayer. In fact, they move automatically from prayer into action, getting up off their knees to participate energetically in the answers to their own prayers.

Naomi prays that God will bless her daughters-in-law with new husbands (Ruth 1:9). And in chapter 3 she will take the initiative in finding a husband for Ruth. She prays for God to bless Boaz for his generosity to two widows in dire straits, and her subsequent selfless actions rain down God's blessings on him.

Boaz and his workers pray for God to be present among them. Then they conduct themselves in sacrificial, gracious ways that overwhelm Ruth with hard evidence that God is truly present in this field. Boaz prays that God will reward Ruth for her kindness to Naomi and for seeking shelter under his wing. Immediately after, he pours his own energies into filling Ruth's arms with grain and prospering her efforts. Boaz blesses her again at the threshing floor when once again he takes up her cause. Subsequently, he becomes a powerful advocate to secure the very blessings for her he has prayed for God to give. Ultimately, this man of prayer becomes *himself* part of the reward he seeks for Ruth as he spreads his wing over her.

More often than not when we dust for God's fingerprints, we come up with the prints of one of his image bearers. Is God working in the fields of Bethlehem? Yes, but what is visible to our eyes is Ruth, bending over the cut grain, and Boaz and his workers making sure she gets as much as she can carry. But the story contains even more powerful and touching evidences of God's hand at work through his image bearers.

Whose Fingerprints?

It may seem disappointing that God doesn't give an audible answer to Naomi's accusation that he has turned against her. That doesn't mean God is silent. It's hard to imagine that a book in the Bible would raise such disturbing questions about God—the very questions we will be asking sooner or later ourselves—and then let the matter drop. God doesn't let it drop. Naomi voices the questions, and God gives his answers loudly and clearly.

God speaks to Naomi through Ruth. The young Moabitess doesn't make long religious speeches or quote Bible verses to her distraught mother-in-law. Naomi probably wouldn't have heard her if she did. Ruth simply lives out her faith in Yahweh and her love for Naomi, a combination that produces a steadfast and sacrificial activism for her mother-in-law's good. In the process, God speaks hope to Naomi's despairing soul through Ruth.

On the road from Moab, when Naomi was feeling utterly forgotten and forsaken by God, she was enfolded in the warm embrace of her daughter-in-law—a physical, tangible reminder that God was holding Naomi fast and would never let her go. Instead of the stony silence of God's rejection, Naomi was hearing resolute words of allegiance—an impassioned oath of covenant love. God was speaking to Naomi, but the voice belonged to her daughter-in-law. "Don't urge me to leave you or to turn back from you. Where you go I will go, and where you stay I will stay" (Ruth 1:16).

Ruth embodied God's *hesed* for Naomi. Her words expressed God's unbreakable bond with his grieving Naomi. In Bethlehem, while Naomi felt desolate and forgotten at home, Ruth was toiling and boldly taking risks in the fields to bring her a meal of roasted grain for today and a sack of raw barley for tomorrow. And Boaz and his workers were going out of their way to make sure that she took home more than she needed.

Little by little, God gets through. Naomi hears *his* voice, feels *his* touch, and is revived by *his* love—not in some supernatural ecstatic epiphany but through the voices, hands, and *hesed* of his image bearers. As she dusts her broken life for God's fingerprints, she discovers Ruth's and Boaz's and the prints of many others.

THE BIRTH OF A BLESSED ALLIANCE

Three lives are intersecting in what is truly a historic moment for God's kingdom—a wounded soldier, a fresh recruit, and a man of valor who does not rest on his laurels. God has deployed all three into active duty, bringing them together in what is one of the most extraordinary examples of a Blessed Alliance that you will find anywhere in Scripture. Naomi brings the light of the gospel to Ruth that draws the Moabitess out of darkness to embrace Naomi's God. Ruth's life is changed forever. And Ruth, despite her own grief, quickly mobilizes to look for new and better ways to fight for Naomi's interests. Ruth lives the gospel. She is an *ezer*-warrior for God's kingdom. She pours herself out for

Naomi, courageously crossing all sorts of social and cultural boundaries to secure Naomi's good.

Ruth's boldness jars the respectable Boaz out of his religious comfort zone and leads him to a more radical, self-sacrificing life of faith—a life that breaks the rules of conventional religion—-just as Jesus, their descendant, will do generations later. The combined efforts of Ruth and Boaz lift a defeated Naomi back to her feet where she joins them by doing some radical gospel living of her own. There is an amazing synergy among the three, and the trio grows deeper in their faith in Yahweh and more outward in their determination to bless the lives of others. The activism of this powerful threesome is about to shake up an entire community and the repercussions will be felt well beyond their culture and time. This powerful alliance will revolutionize their present circumstances and will literally change the world.

A GOD-THING?

Although my own heart is heavy with grief as I write these words, I find Naomi's struggles strangely comforting. Kelly's death draws me to her story, as do other heartaches too personal to mention. How I long for a happy resolution to my troubles so that I can joyously proclaim, "It was a God-thing." Instead, I am left in the silence, watching circumstances unravel, with grief weighing on my heart.

I'm glad Naomi was so honest, for it frees me to be honest too. She lets me know I'm not alone when I wrestle with doubts, don't sense God's love, and can't imagine why he doesn't step in with power to fix today's troubles and bring a happier tomorrow. Like Naomi, I too am earthbound. I can only see where I am at the moment. I don't know how my story will turn out or how these painful pieces fit into the whole.

But Naomi is the wisest of teachers. She doesn't mentor me with a fairy-tale approach to life or a sunny-side-up version of Christianity that is bound to break down sooner or later. Instead, she offers a stark realism that faces head-on the awful tragedies and sorrows of this world. Angry and grief stricken as she is, Naomi's message isn't one of despair but of hope. She displays a grasping faith in Yahweh that clings tenaciously to what is true about him in the swirling cauldron of the worst that life has to offer.

She is in unspeakable pain. Her losses cannot be mended or compensated. There is no cure to make her forget or fully heal from the grief she must carry to her grave. Yet in the midst of her Job-like sufferings, she reaches out with one hand to grasp firmly God's *hesed*, and with the other hand she clasps his providence in her life. He has not stopped nor ever will stop loving her. His *hesed* will pursue her all the days of her life and remains in full force to this day. He is the God of the living and of the dead.

The story doesn't end here, of course. Naomi has been overwhelmed with the surprises Ruth brought home. Now Naomi has a surprise of her own, something Boaz failed to mention: "That man is our close relative; he is one of our kinsman-redeemers [*go'el*]" (Ruth 2:20). This revelation identifies Boaz with a class of individuals in an extended family who were responsible to make sure family land didn't fall into the hands of outsiders. This costly responsibility involved major financial investment—a sacrifice we'll learn more about in subsequent chapters. For now, suffice it to say that Ruth is paying attention. She promptly pockets this vital tidbit of information about Boaz, along with other pieces of legal information she has been collecting from her mother-in-law's comments. She will pull them all out when the moment is right.

DISCUSSION QUESTIONS

1. Describe a situation or event in your life that you would describe as "a God-thing."

2. Why do we tend to restrict God's involvement in our lives to the positive things that happen?

3. What was Naomi's view of God's providence and why was this the heart of her struggle with him?

4. What is providence?

5. How do our prayers and our actions relate to God's providence?

6. How was God speaking to Naomi through Ruth, Boaz, and the harvesters?

7. Why is it important to hang on to *both* God's providence and his *hesed*, no matter what our circumstances?

8. How does God's providence give you hope in troubling circumstances?

Chapter Seven

A HOLY RISK TAKER

He had a classic case of cold feet.

BBC Radio sounded in the background as I was cleaning our Oxford flat. An actor was reading one of Maeve Binchy's short stories[1] about a couple on the eve of their wedding day. Bridal attendants, relatives, and other guests were arriving from out of town. After months of planning and expense, final details were all in order, and the big day was just hours away. Flowers had arrived, and the church looked lovely. The bride had only herself to prepare. She was looking forward to a long hot bath and a restful sleep. And now this. Her fiancé, sitting across from her, was ashen-faced and fumbling for words. She could hardly believe her ears. He was backing out. I stopped what I was doing and sat down on the sofa to listen.

There was nothing she could do. He just couldn't go forward. To save face, she persuaded him to let *her* be the one who didn't show up for the wedding. Relieved that she was taking it so well, the young man agreed. Under the circumstances, it was the least he could do. Next day, as promised, when the wedding march struck up, he solemnly took his place at the front of the church with his best man and the rector. The doors in the back swung open, and all eyes (including his) turned to look. I held my breath. The reader continued, "There she was, coming down the aisle, perfectly at ease on her father's arm and as beautiful a bride as anyone could imagine."

The couple didn't discuss what happened until sometime later on their honeymoon, but the upshot was that she knew him better than he knew himself. The experience no doubt put him on notice that there was a good chance she'd outsmart him again in future situations where they didn't see eye to eye.

Boaz got cold feet too, although the chill he felt was more from the cool night air than from a case of nerves. That isn't to say his nerves didn't get a jolt—just that nerves didn't influence his behavior. In one of the most intriguing (and also comical, when you think about it) scenes in the Bible, Boaz—a buttoned-down man of impeccable conduct—awakens in the middle of the night to discover a woman lying at his feet. No doubt it's an understatement to say he was jolted. There probably aren't words to describe his shock at the awful predicament he was in, and it would be worth a lot to have seen the look on his face.

On the particular night in question, Boaz was a man at rest. The storyteller has fast forwarded about seven weeks[2] through both the barley and wheat harvests, bringing us to scenes surrounding the winnowing of the grain.[3] After this year's harvest, Boaz's quarterly reports are looking good. His accounts are in the black. His workers are paid, and he has even extended his hand to the poor. All season long, he has done everything according to the book. The threshing floor where he is sleeping is heaped with piles of winnowed grain—evidence of a successful crop, lots of hard work, and of God's good bounty. With painful memories still fresh in his mind of the Bethlehem famine that once devastated his land, Boaz is a grateful man.

Ah, the well-deserved rest that comes to such a man. He has feasted merrily with his workers and is now slumbering peacefully on the threshing floor (presumably with one eye open to guard his grain). And now this. The silhouette of a woman next to him in the darkness has alarm bells going off in his head. Just wait until Bethlehem tabloids catch wind of this! This man of valor can easily imagine this private moment leading to a public fall from grace, no matter what happens next. Suddenly wide awake, Boaz whispers hoarsely in the darkness, "Who are you?" (Ruth 3:9).

A FEMALE CONSPIRACY?

In addition to being humorous, this midnight threshing floor scene is also one of the most powerful gospel encounters between two people in all of Scripture. But the power has been drained from the story because we are so distracted by our uncertainty over what Naomi intended to happen when she sent Ruth to Boaz that night and by our concern over what Ruth actually did when she uncovered Boaz's feet.

Was Naomi serving Ruth up on a platter for Boaz to have sex with her that night? Is Ruth being forward and doing something sexually inappropriate? Suspicions abound that she is trying to seduce him, and some think that is exactly what the man needs. For if his romantic interest in Ruth is as genuine and strong as generally supposed, Boaz appears to be a bit of a sluggard as a suitor—slow in making his move and needing women to scheme, cajole, and flirt to force his hand. According to this theory, tonight they have him cornered. Like the unsuspecting groom of Binchy's imagination, Boaz is outfoxed and outmaneuvered by *two* conspiring women who understand him better than he understands himself. They ambush him in the middle of the night to give him what he's wanting anyway.

But surely the book of Ruth was written for better reasons than to portray men as dullards or women as conniving seductresses. I find it next to impossible to reconcile the Ruth of episodes one and two with a woman who would stoop to something resembling a *Desperate Housewives* plot to entrap an honorable man like Boaz in a moral dilemma that demands marriage.

Some interpreters express disappointment that a story that begins with such promise for women and presents a refreshing and hopeful picture of strong relationships between the sexes (and all within the patriarchal culture) ends by embracing convention.

Just when we're praising Ruth for her independent spirit and admiring her intelligent, bold leadership among God's people, both she and Naomi revert to the view that a woman's salvation comes through a man, marriage, and motherhood.

As if to make matters worse, in the concluding chapter Ruth disappears from her own story. Everyone is talking *about* her. No one talks to her, nor is her voice heard again. What we're seeing seems to reinforce the notion that women must be strong leaders in the absence of a man (and may actually have no choice), but once he's back on the scene, they can recede into the background again.

The Past Invades the Present

This, of course, is where it helps to remember that God is still the main hero of the story. The Bible (including this strange and mysterious episode) centers on revealing him and his transforming work in human hearts. There is deep theology in this chapter too, but we have to wade through some murky issues to begin to see it. Questions we face in this scene underscore why we need to keep reminding ourselves that each new episode in this story is deeply embedded in what has gone before.

Naomi, despite her remarkable recovery, is still in a lot of pain. And Ruth has not forgotten the pledge she made to her mother-in-law back on the road connecting Moab to Bethlehem. Even here with Boaz, her vow continues to be the driving force behind her choices and her actions. She worked diligently through the barley and the wheat harvests—close behind the maids of Boaz—to make sure Naomi has plenty to eat in the present and a well-stocked larder for the long winter ahead. But they are still in poverty, still putting one foot in front of the other in their efforts to survive. Ruth will bring as much energy, resourcefulness, devotion to Naomi, and out-of-the-box thinking to this new challenge as she has to everything else.

As for Boaz, his interactions with Ruth so far have only served to enhance his standing in the community. If anything, he stands even taller in Bethlehem now as both a man of valor and a man of uncommon generosity. We thought a lot of him when we first met him. Now that we've seen him voluntarily aiding Ruth's efforts to take care of Naomi, we respect him even more. So whatever questions and uncertainties we bring to the current episode, our understanding of what happens next must factor in what we've already observed in the character and behavior of each of these three individuals up to this point.

In Search of Rest

The mystery shrouding the encounter between Ruth and Boaz at the threshing floor is heightened by the fact that Naomi is the instigator. Not only has she reemerged from her despondency, her mind is now engaged in matters beyond the narrow circumference of her own sorrow. Reassured by the knowledge that Yahweh's *hesed* is still at work in her life, Naomi is freed from self-absorption. Her thoughts turn to Ruth and the future as she zeros in on a serious problem that she alone can address.

If life follows the normal trajectory, there's a high likelihood that Ruth will outlive her Israelite mother-in-law. And then, what will become of Ruth? A foreign widow all alone in Bethlehem? Life may be difficult for them now, but without Naomi, difficulties will escalate for the Moabitess. The widows of Vrindavan gave us a sobering picture of the perils faced by the woman who is disconnected, uneducated, and unskilled. Add to that a foreigner's status, and the complications multiply. There will be no rest for Ruth. But Naomi does more than think about these problems. Revived in faith, Naomi becomes an activist too. She joins the ranks of *hesed*-givers as she sheds her passivity and takes charge of the action for the sake of her daughter-in-law.

A woman's only viable option for security in Naomi's day was the one she mentioned en route to Bethlehem when she prayed that Orpah and Ruth would "find rest in the home of another husband" (Ruth 1:9). Within the ancient culture, and certainly in Naomi's mind, marriage was a practical matter—a place of safety, security, and rest from the perils and poverty of widowhood. Naomi herself is doomed to a life of unrest, but that doesn't prevent her from taking steps to secure rest for her son's widow. If her plan succeeds, Ruth will marry Boaz, and Naomi will go to her grave in peace, knowing her daughter-in-law has found safe haven.

In Moab, Ruth's family could and no doubt would take up this responsibility. Now that she is in Bethlehem, things are significantly more complicated. For starters, men (usually fathers and brothers) negotiated marriages. There is no man to speak for Ruth — another painful reminder that the widow has no voice. Even if there was a man to advocate on Ruth's behalf, she has no bargaining power at all — no dowry, no social connections, no political advantages to bring to the table. Contrary to our Western tendency to place romance above all other considerations when it comes to the choice of a marriage partner, in Naomi's day marriages cemented strategic alliances for families — securing important social, economic, and political benefits and the promise of progeny. Based on the culture's standards for evaluating prospective brides, Ruth was out of luck. Worst of all, her foreign ancestry and long history of barrenness added a double-negative to her deficiencies.

These obstacles do not deter Naomi, who now exhibits the same gutsy, rule-breaking mentality we've seen in Ruth. Naomi will bend the rules and work around the system to secure the husband Ruth needs. The plan she hatches is simply brilliant and no doubt would have worked like a charm. Only Naomi didn't count on the fact that her daughter-in-law would break a few rules herself, beginning with her mother-in-law's instructions.

Naomi Unveils Her Plan

Naomi's plan is simple, although not without great risk to Ruth's person and reputation if the strategy backfires. Most mothers and mothers-in-law would recoil at the thought of sending a defenseless young woman out alone into the night, much less into a surprise rendezvous with a sleeping man in an area where there has been feasting and drinking and who knows what else.[4] Naomi is acutely aware of the risks, but in her mind they are worth taking if they result in sparing Ruth from the darkening future ahead. Naomi has come up with the plan that is most likely to succeed, despite the inherent dangers.

She begins by identifying Boaz as the prospective groom. She chooses him, *not* because she's noticed that he fancies Ruth, but (according to her own words) because of their connections with him. He is the man in whose fields Ruth has been working (i.e., he is a known entity who has already demonstrated a gracious heart), and he is a relative or kinsman—which gives him reason to care (Ruth 3:2). Naomi is not recklessly throwing her daughter-in-law to the proverbial wolves. She sensitively and wisely selects a man whose godly character is known and whom Ruth has had plenty of opportunity to observe. Naomi is also banking a lot on the fact that Ruth is not unknown to Boaz, and his conduct toward her daughter-in-law reinforces Naomi's hope that he will respond favorably.

To overcome the lack of a male go-between, Ruth must approach Boaz herself. But even here, the older widow has done her homework. Naomi is a master strategist. She has figured out the perfect time and place for a private conversation with Boaz that will not impugn Ruth or Boaz if her scheme fails. She knows where Boaz will be that evening, what he will be doing, when his mood will be most favorable, and what will be the best manner and most propitious moment to approach him. Boaz will be winnowing grain[5] at the threshing floor tonight.[6] After feasting he will spend the night there guarding his grain. He will be alone, and the night will provide the privacy such an encounter requires.

Naomi instructs Ruth to prepare herself by bathing, anointing herself with perfumed oil, and putting on her best garments. Some think Ruth was dressing as a bride, which is entirely possible. At the very least she is breaking out of her identity as a widow and ending her time of mourning. Frederic Bush believes that by removing the symbols and garments of widowhood, Ruth is "indicating her intention of engaging once again in the normal activities and relationships of life. She is thus available for the marriage that Naomi seeks for her."[7]

Naomi directs Ruth to go to the threshing floor under cover of darkness, wait until Boaz finishes eating, and note carefully where he lies down for the night. It will be disastrous if in the darkness Ruth approaches the wrong man. Boaz will be in good spirits, full of contentment and satisfaction over the work accomplished—a ready target for Ruth's approach. Naomi gives her final instructions: "Go and uncover his feet and lie down. He will tell you what to do" (Ruth 3:4).

By following Naomi's directions, Ruth will send nonverbal signals to Boaz that marriage is in view—a widow coming out of mourning, perfume in the air, the uncovering of a sleeping man's feet or legs, and her posture as a petitioner at his feet. Boaz will be in no doubt of what Ruth is proposing. At the same time, she is making herself exceedingly vulnerable. Daniel Block describes Naomi's plan as "fraught with danger," and her proposal of marriage as "highly irregular from the standpoint of custom: a woman propositioning a man; a young person propositioning an older person; a destitute field worker propositioning the land-owner."[8] Once again suspense revolves around how Boaz will respond. Naomi places extraordinary trust in Boaz and takes a deep breath as she braces for another anxious all-night vigil.

So Far So Good

Everything goes perfectly according to plan. Scrubbed and scented and freed of her widow's garb, Ruth covertly makes her way to the threshing floor. Hidden in the shadows, she watches as Boaz finishes eating and drinking, then settles himself in the darkness for a peaceful night of rest. She waits. After a strenuous day of harvest activity, weary harvesters make their way back to the village or disperse to spaces on the threshing floor and arrange themselves for the night. Then all is quiet, except for the gentle whisper of the breeze, perhaps an occasional snore, and the pounding of Ruth's heart.

The time has come to act. With the stealth of a cat burglar, Ruth rises cautiously and moves without a sound to the place where Boaz lies sleeping, uncovers his feet, lies down, and waits to see what will happen next. She has followed Naomi's instructions to the letter—and we want to know what on earth she did.

Clearly, the storyteller has loaded the story with sexual overtones. Language full of double-meanings, the isolated setting, a man and a woman alone in the darkness, Ruth uncovering Boaz's "feet"—all combine to create an aura of ambiguity intended to leave the reader wondering how much of Boaz she uncovers and what Boaz will do with this interesting and unexpected opportunity when he wakes up.[9] Clearly they are in a sexually charged situation.

Although Hebrew scholars I consulted tend to think that Ruth simply uncovered Boaz's feet or legs and waited for the cool night air to awaken him, we simply do not know exactly what she did. But here's what we do know. Naomi's intentions are upright and her whole purpose is to secure Ruth's safety, not to jeopardize her future. She has taken the greatest care to avoid tarnishing Ruth's reputation and is sending her to a man she has every reason to believe will not exploit the situation to his own advantage but will receive her daughter-in-law with respect and honor.

We also know that Ruth and Boaz have both exhibited unusual levels of godly character, and we expect no less from either of them here. They are followers of Yahweh. They live under his gaze. Their actions are motivated by *hesed*, and they are willing to make great personal sacrifices to live faithfully for him—*particularly* in how they relate to others. Ruth will do nothing to compromise Boaz, especially not knowing his answer. And his response to her actions gives solid evidence that her conduct has in no way crossed the line, dishonored him, or forced him into marriage.

The narrator has deliberately created a scene riddled with sexual tension, *not* to spice up the story for the sake of sensationalism, but to drive home an important point—namely, that Yahweh's people are perpetually confronted with difficult situations and hard choices. Will they be guided by self-interest or will *hesed* cause them to set aside self-interest and freely sacrifice for others? In every episode of the book of Ruth, one or more of the central characters face that kind of decision, and we repeatedly observe them going above and beyond what duty, custom, and the law require. These are gospel moments—glimpses of the kind of world God envisioned at creation and that Jesus came to restore. Scholar Edward F. Campbell Jr. elaborates:

> What now happens at the threshing floor is as essential to the story-teller's purpose as what happened on the Moabite highway between Ruth and Naomi, or what happened in the harvest scene when Boaz praised an impoverished widow who was gleaning, or what will happen in the solemn civil hearing at the city gate. At each of these points in the story, a moment of choice is presented to both actors and audience, and at each of these points the choice is made in favor of what righteous living calls for.[10]

MIDNIGHT DEBACLE

Boaz shivers in the cold, stirs, and wakes to find a woman at his feet. This is the moment when Ruth surprises everyone by tossing Naomi's script and improvising with a script of her own. Instead of waiting (as Naomi intended) for Boaz to grasp the nature of her unspoken petition and tell her what to do, Ruth identifies herself, then instructs Boaz to "spread your covering [your wing] over your maid, for you are a close relative [go'el]" (Ruth 3:9, NASB). Ruth's language beautifully alludes to Boaz's earlier description of her taking shelter under Yahweh's wings (2:12). Now she seeks shelter under Boaz's wing—imagery he clearly understands as a request for marriage.

However, her unexpected departure from Naomi's carefully scripted mission throws a wrench into the works. Ruth addresses Boaz, not with a simple appeal to marry a destitute widow, but by confronting him with his legal responsibilities as a near relative of Elimelech. Now, instead of a simple private transaction between two people and a marriage that could have been consummated that night (which seems to have been Naomi's expectation),[11] this becomes a public legal matter with serious complications involving other parties. In a few words, Naomi's plan is overthrown, and everything is changed.

Some think Ruth is naïve and uninformed, that she makes a terrible gaffe when she tangles up two important but separate family laws that she has heard her mother-in-law mention—the levirate law and the law of the kinsman-redeemer. They think in his response, Boaz is just being polite and trying to smooth things over, that his words are "calculated to remove the embarrassment of the situation—to cover Ruth's *faux pas*."[12] Based on what we've seen of Ruth so far, I'm inclined to disagree. We'll look into that more in the next chapter. But for our purposes here, what are the laws that she invokes?

ANCIENT FAMILY LAWS

In every Israelite family, two issues were paramount: the survival of the family name and keeping family land in family hands. The Elimelech family ran into trouble on both counts. Famine drove them off their land, and the deaths of Elimelech and his two sons threaten the family with extinction. Mosaic Law, however, carried provisions to save a dying family and to protect their ownership of their land.

The levirate law addressed the situation where a man died without an heir. Under this law, *his brother* was required to marry and impregnate his widow. The son born from this union would carry forward the line of the deceased. As an added benefit, the widow would be sheltered.[13] This was the duty of a brother-in-law, and great shame and dishonor fell on the man who refused to fulfill this family obligation.

The kinsman-redeemer law focused on the land and encompassed a wider range of relatives. When a man fell onto hard times and was forced to sell his land, his *nearest relative* (or kinsman-redeemer) was called to step in and purchase the land (or buy it back from an outsider) to keep his relative's property from coming under the ownership of someone outside their tribe.[14]

Both laws were costly and involved enormous sacrifice. Since a father's estate was divided among his sons, when one son died childless, the surviving brothers' inheritance automatically increased. The family pie was sliced into fewer (and therefore larger) pieces. According to levirate law, the brother whose duty it was to marry the widow was spoiling his own inheritance if he succeeded in fathering a son by her. The newborn would replace his deceased brother—and those lovely larger pieces of pie would shrink in size again because now there was one more heir to include in dividing family property. According to these calculations, becoming your brother's keeper is a losing proposition. But it is the *hesed*-way of doing things.

The kinsman-redeemer faced a similar conflict of interest, for rescuing his relatives' property involved the outlay of large sums of money.[15] In the process of redeeming his relative's land, the kinsman-redeemer was siphoning off financial resources from his own estate, so his sons would inherit less. The law wasn't simply a legal code, but a heart-piercing call to a higher way of living. It was a call to sacrifice. It is the gospel in the Old Testament.

THE MYSTERY SURROUNDING BOAZ

Boaz may be stunned by Ruth's presence and the words he has just heard her speak, but he is anything but speechless. Suddenly the script belongs to Boaz. Instead of taking offense or shaming and driving Ruth away into the night, as one might expect, his words are just as surprising as hers. He praises her actions, calls on Yahweh to bless her for what she has done, and links what she is doing to her earlier acts of *hesed*. "The LORD bless you, my daughter.... This kindness [*hesed*] is greater than that which you showed earlier: You have not run after the younger men, whether rich or poor" (Ruth 3:10).

He exonerates her behavior. She was not a man-chaser then, nor is she now. Far from being forward or inappropriate, her bold actions reflect a quality of righteousness that inspires an outpouring of praise from this highly esteemed man. And Boaz isn't a victim of underhanded schemes, manipulation, or entrapment either. According to his interpretation of what is happening here, Ruth hasn't made a blunder, but knows exactly what she is doing. He sees (and is in awe) that once again, *hesed* is at work, and in this, he is always a willing accomplice.

Students of the book of Ruth often draw attention to the fact that both Naomi and Boaz repeatedly address Ruth as "my daughter."[16] This has led many to conclude that Boaz is an older man and of the same generation as Naomi and Elimelech. For years I thought of Boaz (and heard teaching that portrayed him) as unmarried and perhaps a bit like Jane Austen's Mr. Knightly, who was well-off and highly respected, but an older bachelor who for some unknown reason just hadn't gotten around to marriage. But the more I've learned about patriarchal cultures such as you find in today's Middle East, the more aware I am that my conclusions have been largely shaped by my Western views of relationships between men and women and are wide of the mark.

In the ancient Israelite society, it simply wasn't possible to combine the levels of honor and stature that Boaz clearly possessed with the postponement of marriage or the absence of sons. It's hard for those of us in the West to comprehend just how much hinges on producing sons in other societies, but in fact the very foundations and survival of many cultures depend on each generation's success in producing a whole new crop of sons.

A central thesis of the book of Ruth is the utter necessity of sons. Israelite parents would be desperately wringing their hands over a son who neglected this primary family duty, no matter how successful he happened to be in other arenas. The family had no future without sons. Instead of being a man of valor, Boaz would be a disgrace and grief to his family if he had no sons. And instead of admiration, the whole community would show pity toward him. In her insightful book on contemporary Middle Eastern culture, journalist Geraldine Brooks reveals the intense shame borne by a Palestinian man whose wife failed to produce a son. Utterly humiliated and frantic for a second wife, the man conceded bitterly, "I am nothing in this village without a son."[17]

When it comes to personal demographics, Boaz is something of a mystery man, and the narrator doesn't fill in the blanks. We don't know if Boaz had a living wife, or two or three, or if he was a widower. But to the early readers of this story, it really didn't matter, for in ancient Israelite society polygamy was both common and accepted. Abraham, Jacob, and David are but a few significant examples of notable polygamists. In the eyes of that culture, a man with multiple wives was following an appropriate strategy (even a necessary one) for producing many sons, regardless of the negative repercussions in individual lives. It was also, oddly enough, something of a mercy for women, for it shielded them from the kinds of adversities Naomi and Ruth were suffering. We cannot know for sure whether Ruth's proposal involved polygamy, but given the culture and Boaz's age, it is almost certain he had sons of his own and their inheritance to consider when contemplating Ruth's petition. This fact alone raises the stakes for the decision facing Boaz.

THE GOSPEL INVADES THE PRESENT

If you're at all like me, you find this discussion deeply unsettling, not just because this seems to spoil how we've viewed the relationship between Ruth and Boaz, but also because we're talking about the cultural setting of the Bible. I end up trying to sift out the good from the bad in an effort to understand how God expects us to live together in this world. I'll throw out polygamy and slavery, of course, but it all seems so confusing. What elements of the ancient culture are we supposed to preserve?

Jesus' announcement that "my kingdom is not of this world" should alert us to expect that the culture God intends to establish in this earth is nothing like the human cultures the world has witnessed so far. The biblical story is told against the backdrop of fallen human culture. This backdrop is *not* the Bible's message, but serves to intensify that message.

For example, understanding culture's extremely high view of sons helps us begin to grasp the unspeakably great sacrifice God made when he gave his one and only well-beloved Son to redeem a fallen world. But, lest we assume from this that the Bible is embracing a high view of sons and a low view of daughters, the apostle Paul circles around and elevates women to full status in God's family by announcing, "*You are all sons* of God through faith in Christ Jesus" (Galatians 3:26, emphasis added). The kingdom God intends to establish on earth is a kingdom where both sons and daughters are held at a premium, *hesed* is our mode of operation, and Jesus defines the paradigm for our relationships.

So, although reading our Bibles takes us into the ancient patriarchal culture, a system that devalued women, the Bible simultaneously introduces laws to regulate that system and to protect the weakest members of society and (more importantly) systematically undermines and dismantles the ethics that drive that system. We find one of the best examples of this in the story before us. The gospel takes us to a completely different realm of human relations. Here, at the threshing floor in the exchange between Boaz and Ruth, we catch a glimpse of how that kingdom is supposed to look. She presses for *hesed*. And he not only joins her cause once again, he takes an active role in overthrowing the culture's views of women in the words he speaks to Ruth.

THE MEASURE OF A WOMAN

Words of kindness, praise, and reassurance flow from Boaz's mouth. "And now, my daughter, don't be afraid. I will do for you all you ask" (Ruth 3:11). Then he proceeds to turn the ancient patriarchal value system completely upside down. Ruth is a barren, impoverished, foreign widow—worthless in that society's eyes. Boaz overturns that verdict by attaching the highest possible value to her simply for herself as a person. It is a major break from the ancient culture, but one the whole community supports. "All my fellow townsmen know that you are a woman of noble character" (3:11).

This is a stunning moment in the biblical record—one with seismic ramifications for women. It is yet another instance in Scripture where we see that gospel living goes against the grain of human culture. Boaz foreshadows how Jesus would one day reach out to women who were rejected by their communities, to commission and empower them to serve him. The Samaritan woman, Mary Magdalene, and his own mother are just a few prominent examples.

What stuns me even more is the fact that Boaz uses the same Hebrew word (*ḥayil*) for Ruth that the narrator used earlier to describe him as a man of valor—"the elite warrior similar to the hero of the Homeric epic."[18] Some Bible translators downsize the word to "noble character" or "excellence" here in reference to Ruth. Not so fast, say Hebrew experts. "When the term is used of a woman (Ruth 3:11; Prov. 12:4; and 31:10)[19] it is translated 'virtuous' (ASV, RSV 'worthy' or 'good') but it may well be that a woman of this caliber had all the attributes of her male counterpart."[20] I think Boaz would agree. Ruth is, after all, an *ezer*, fighting valiantly to rescue the Elimelech family line.

Just when everything is going better than anyone imagined, Boaz breaks the news that Ruth has indeed approached the wrong man. He is not the nearest relative. There is one who is nearer and has first responsibility as kinsman-redeemer to the Elimelech family. Boaz must step aside. However, Boaz has a back-up plan if the nearer relative opts out—Boaz pledges, and calls Yahweh to be his witness, that he will surely marry Ruth.

The existence of a nearer kinsman adds a whole new layer of suspense to the story. We are pulling for Boaz. But this nearer relative has a prior claim and eliminates Boaz (at least for the moment). Boaz intends to handle the matter first thing in the morning. It was too late for Ruth to return to Bethlehem without risking both of their reputations. So Boaz instructs Ruth to lie down and sleep until morning.

SLEEPLESS IN BETHLEHEM

I doubt if either Boaz or Ruth got any sleep at all, with so much on their minds and the uncertainties of the next day. And now for sure Boaz must keep an eye open, for what would happen if someone stumbled over them in the night? No doubt Naomi was tossing and turning in her bed too, wondering whether her mission had succeeded.

Early the next morning, before dawn, Naomi heard the sound of footsteps approaching her door. Ruth is home again—not as a married woman, as Naomi had hoped, but with a large gift

Boaz sent for Naomi, a *seah* of grain, which scholars estimate ran anywhere from sixty to a hundred pounds.[21] The gift reassures Naomi that Boaz honors her daughter-in-law's request and will handle everything on their behalf. As Ruth explains everything that happened to Naomi, Boaz is already heading for Bethlehem's gate, where he will keep his word. He may have had cold feet in the night, but as the morning breaks across the Judean horizon his heart is deeply warmed by *hesed*.

We will hear no more from Ruth, although she figures largely in the final episode. The rest of the story will be told by Boaz and by Naomi. But we have lots of questions about what went wrong this night. Why did Ruth veer off course from Naomi's plan? Why was Boaz impressed instead of shocked by her conduct? And was it really okay for the women to take the initiative, especially in proposing marriage? How are we supposed to reconcile a woman's call to be submissive with the kind of behavior we've witnessed here in both of the heroines of this story? We'll examine these questions next.

DISCUSSION QUESTIONS

1. Describe a situation where you had to do something difficult, but you knew it was the right thing to do. What gave you courage (or prevented you from stepping out) to address the problem?

2. What changes do you observe in Naomi? How do you explain her newfound courage and determination to help Ruth?

3. What do you think of Naomi's plan? Why was it so risky?

4. Why was Boaz the perfect choice for a husband for Ruth? What were the risks in approaching him?

5. Why wasn't he offended by Ruth's proposal?

6. What impressed Boaz most about Ruth and caused him to value her so highly?

7. How do Boaz's words to Ruth change our understanding of a woman's true value? How is this different from other messages we hear?

8. How do Naomi's and Ruth's evolving relationships with Yahweh point us to the true source of courage and strength and guide our steps when addressing difficult situations in our lives?

Chapter Eight

THE THREE FACES
OF SUBMISSION

"Shouldn't we be teaching our daughters to be more compliant?"

The question came from the back row in a seminar on Christian marriage. The topic under discussion that day was a wife's submission to her husband, and the concerned dad who raised the question had good reason to ask. His teenage daughters were gifted, highly motivated honor students who were ready to take on the world. Would they make good wives if they didn't start practicing how to submit to the leadership of men? Were they cultivating skills, attitudes, and qualities that could sabotage their chances of a healthy and successful Christian marriage? Already he could see his strong daughters might need a little coaching and perhaps a bit of reining in.

When we heard the question, Frank and I exchanged glances. We were thinking the same thing. A girl with a compliant spirit is dangerously ill-prepared for life in today's world of sexual violence against women. Attending the marriage seminar that day were parents of Christian daughters who had been date-raped, some by boys who were active in their youth group. There were also women present whose respectable Christian leader husbands had, behind closed doors, physically pushed them around or worse.

Statistics that do not include unreported incidents tell us one in five female high school students has been physically and/or sexually abused by a date partner[1] and that one out of four adult women has suffered at least one incident of physical violence in marriage. In a 2007 briefing paper to the United Nations Commission on the Status of Women, World Vision included this chilling statement, "The majority of the world's women and girls will experience violence; whether it's physical, psychological or sexual violence, it plagues every community and many homes."[2]

Even Christian parents who are mindful of such dangers promote female submission, not as a potential danger but as a benefit to Christian marriage. I once heard a man explain how submission worked in his marriage, revealing what he believed was a more moderate approach to the subject. "Usually, submission isn't an issue for us," he began. "Most of the time my wife and I agree. But on those rare occasions when we don't, then I ask her to submit." Submission, from his perspective, is the great tiebreaker, which, when given by a wife, keeps the peace in many households as a workable formula for resolving marital deadlocks. Like the fire extinguisher collecting dust in the closet, his version of submission remains conveniently within reach in case of emergency and quickly puts out sparks that if left unchecked might burst into flame.

Sometimes, however, this so-called tiebreaker leaves a woman smoldering with resentment. One woman, for whom a single act of wifely submission came at the price of a lifelong dream, secretly resented her unbending husband for years. Another young wife (who evidently hadn't yet mastered the art of giving in), when asked a few months after her wedding how married life suited her, admitted feeling "oppressed, repressed, suppressed, and depressed."

In all of the confusion, it is tempting to side with those who are convinced that submission is an outdated convention—okay for previous generations perhaps, but passé in today's world. Like the Amish horse-drawn buggies traveling on modern roads in Pennsylvania's beautiful Lancaster County, submission is a relic from a bygone era. Asking a woman to submit to her husband represents an unwillingness to move forward, a refusal to wake up to how the world around us is changing for women or to accept advances that make life better for everyone. People who insist on clinging to submission for women are simply stuck in the past at best. And there are plenty of single women who wonder why any woman would want to marry if submission is the price of admission.

Yet when I open my Bible, I see a New Testament call to submission addressed to me as a Christian and as a woman. I'd like to believe it isn't so, but there it is in black and white. Advocates on both sides of the discussion express concern over the abuses. At the same time, there's no getting around the fact that the Bible clearly teaches submission. How do we reconcile this teaching with the brutal realities of our fallen world? Are we left to look for a kinder, gentler version of submission? Or does the Bible's version of submission (which surprisingly addresses *both* men and women) take us to a whole new realm of human relationships, just as *hesed* does? Do our definitions of submission actually trivialize what it really means?

THE TROUBLE WITH RUTH

I suppose an entire book could be written on the subject of submission, and if the confusion I've just described is at all representative of the climate in Christian circles, someone needs to take up that task. My purpose here, however, is not to set forth an exhaustive treatment of the subject, but to talk about how submission relates to the story of Ruth. Often, when we think of godly, submissive women, Ruth comes to mind as something of an icon of submissiveness. Yet it's difficult to reconcile the different versions of submission we've been considering with the behavior we see when we look closely at Ruth.

Not that I don't see what people are talking about when they point to Ruth as the quintessential submissive woman. Certainly she consistently honors and respects both Naomi and Boaz. She consults with Naomi before going to glean and heeds her council by staying with Boaz's maids through the harvest season. She conforms to the conventions of her day when she approaches the master of the field with her petition for special gleaning privileges and in bowing to the ground to thank him for his kindness. She offers unflinching obedience to Naomi's shocking directives regarding a midnight rendezvous with Boaz. "Everything you have said I will do" (Ruth 3:5–6, Hubbard translation). But Boaz says the same thing to Ruth when she proposes marriage to him at the threshing floor. "Everything you have said, I will do for you" (Ruth 3:11, Hubbard translation). And aren't we taking things a bit far to link the kind of submission the Bible advocates with Ruth's offer of herself to Boaz at the threshing floor?

What is more, portraying Ruth as the icon of submissiveness puts her in conflict with herself. One moment she is deferential and respectful of her elders. In the next she is gutsy, bold, and assertively breaking the rules. Yet her unconventional ideas and radical behavior win the admiration of Naomi and Boaz who are confronted, nonplussed, and blessed by her unpredictable ways. In fact the whole community is singing her praises. Which is the real Ruth? Does the kind of submission advocated in the Bible conflict with Ruth's stronger attributes? Or is biblical submission actually connected to her strengths and worked out in these courageous, voluntary acts of self-sacrifice that we repeatedly see her making?

DRILLING DOWN DEEPER

I started having second thoughts about submission when I was asked to speak on the subject to a group of young single women. It was an interesting assignment, and I thought at the time entirely appropriate (if not actually strategic) to discuss this topic with women before the gate of holy matrimony clicked shut behind them. In search of inspiration, I asked Frank if he could think of a time when I had submitted to him. The room suddenly got quiet as he reflected over what by then was more than a decade of marriage. "No," he replied slowly after a long pause, "I can't think of any."

That wasn't the answer I was expecting. His response triggered a lengthy discussion of our history together. The conversation that followed was an eye-opener for both of us because we realized submission is *not* an occasional event. It is a lifestyle. It isn't a negative obligation on women, but the natural outworking of the gospel in every Christian's life. Submission is an attribute of Jesus, so it ought to show up in all of his followers. We ended up talking about him.

New Testament writers do that too. They never talk about submission without talking about Jesus, and in particular of the cross. Jesus' version of submission is thoughtful, strong, purposeful, and sacrificial. It involves the full and determined embrace of his Father's will (which governs everything Jesus does)[3] and the voluntary pouring out of his life to rescue a lost world.[4] Submission is both. It is redemptive. It is the gospel. It is a way of showing Jesus to the world.

Some may tell you Ruth is doing all the submitting. But submission is apparent in Naomi and in Boaz as well. At points it is impossible to distinguish which of the three is more radical and selfless in living for Yahweh and laying down their life for others. But while the rest of the town lies sleeping, the future invades the present. At the threshing floor, a thin band of light breaks through the blackness of the night as we catch a glimpse of the kingdom Jesus will one day give his life to rebuild. On this holy night in Bethlehem, the gospel is *preenacted* by three people who have never heard of Jesus, but whose words and actions speak unmistakably of him.

THE WIDOW'S MITE

When Naomi sat Ruth down and laid out her plan for approaching Boaz, the general consensus is that she was playing matchmaker. According to this thesis, Naomi kept a watchful eye all through the harvest on the blossoming love between Boaz and her hardworking daughter-in-law. The time had come for action. Boaz needed a bit of encouragement, and Naomi had devised the perfect plan to bring the two lovers together.

Almost everyone agrees that Naomi is genuinely seeking Ruth's happiness. However, most interpreters also believe Naomi sees in this match one last flicker of hope for her family's survival. If Ruth's marriage to Boaz produces a son, the Elimelech family will be saved. And without stopping to consider what this says about Naomi's character — the level of selfishness and insensitivity to Ruth — we move on quickly to the threshing floor to find out what will happen next. The implications, however, reflect badly on Naomi, and we owe it to her to think this through.

The key to understanding Naomi's actions is to listen carefully to her words. Earlier, when she discovered Ruth had been working in Boaz's field, she described him as "one of our *kinsman-redeemers*" (Ruth 2:20, emphasis added) or *go'el*. As we noted before, this technical description identifies Boaz as a family member who has both legal and moral responsibilities to bail Elimelech out of financial trouble if ever he is forced to sell his land. Now, as she sends Ruth to the threshing floor, Naomi doesn't mention his legal relationship to their family. She speaks of Boaz simply as "*a kinsman*" or a relative (3:2).

When Ruth speaks to Boaz in the darkness, however, she employs his legal title and names him as their *go'el*. Clearly Naomi and Ruth are at cross purposes. If Naomi had been thinking of resuscitating the family, she would never have sent Ruth to Boaz, for redemption was not his responsibility, and Naomi certainly knew who was her husband's nearest *go'el*. But her agenda had nothing to do with Elimelech's land. Instead of selfishly using her daughter-in-law for family interests, Naomi is making a sacrifice.

Judging from her words, down-to-earth Naomi is purely motivated by pragmatics. She awakens to the urgent need to find safe haven for Ruth in the home of a husband. "Should I not try to find a home [or rest] for you, where you will be well provided for?" (Ruth 3:1). After Naomi dies, her Moabite daughter-in-law will remain alone in Bethlehem. The thought of this — the deeper hardship and suffering this will impose on Ruth — is unacceptable to Naomi. She may be helpless to prevent it, but she will at least do what she can to spare Ruth from facing the miserable fate of a lonely foreign widow. The only real solution in the ancient patriarchal culture is the protection of a man.

So she sends Ruth to Boaz. His kindnesses to Ruth so far, coupled with the family connections, give Naomi reasons to hope he will find it in his heart to bring Ruth into his household through marriage. Naomi seeks mercy, not offspring. Her objective is security for Ruth, not a child for her family. Naomi has been with Ruth through her long, heartbreaking struggle with barrenness. Anyone who has watched a loved one suffer through the heartache of infertility would never dream of doing anything to reopen that tender wound. As I mentioned before, I suspect this man of high standing in the community was already married and had sons of his own, so we could easily be talking polygamy. But within the ancient patriarchal culture, this was simply how things worked.

The sacrifice Naomi is about to make is staggering by anyone's estimation. She is a grief-stricken woman. She went out full and came back empty. But in the intervening weeks since her return, she has made two amazing discoveries. First, that Yahweh has not forgotten her after all. His *hesed* still surrounds her and is active in her life. And second, as she has watched—day after day—as her daughter-in-law set out to glean, she has come to realize, at some level, that she isn't as empty as she first thought. God has blessed her life with Ruth, who is later aptly described by Naomi's friends as "your daughter-in-law, who loves you" (Ruth 4:15).

Now, in the face of deepening adversity for Ruth, Naomi is willing to give up the only blessing she has, and we must give serious thought to what this will mean for Naomi, who will be left alone.

We are watching Naomi pour herself out for Ruth. This is a powerful act of submission. She is like the poor widow Jesus noticed dropping her last pennies into the temple coffers. In the words of Jesus, "I tell you the truth, this poor widow has put more into the treasury than all the others" (Mark 12:43). Naomi, out of her poverty, is giving away all she has. Even from the dusty rubble of ground zero, she makes a sacrifice. This is the gospel. This is submission. This is how God's kingdom looks on earth.

NOT YOUR MOTHER'S SUBMISSION

The gospel shows up in Ruth's actions too. She is submissive—
more than anyone could imagine. But this is not your mother's
submission, or your grandmother's, for that matter. And we
won't begin to comprehend its richness and power if all we see is
a woman bending low before the master of the field or lying at the
feet of her future husband and do not probe the deeper meaning
of her actions.

One of the biggest mistakes we make in Bible study is to draw
the conclusion that certain women acted in powerful ways yet
were clueless about what they were doing. Naomi sends Ruth
on a mission. We assume Ruth misunderstands her instructions,
that she misinterprets Jewish law and turns an awkward situation
into an embarrassing legal predicament by confronting Boaz with
another man's responsibilities. Yet despite bungling everything,
she ends up marrying the right man, conceiving the right baby,
saving the family, and (wonder of wonders) rescuing the royal line
of David and of Jesus. Like Calamity Jane, Ruth blunders her way
into the perfect ending. It all seems a bit far-fetched to me.

What if this isn't a series of blunders? What if Ruth deliberately tampers with Naomi's script? What if she is doing again
what she's done in every other episode—looking for more and
better ways to love Naomi, showing little regard for her own
future happiness, and probing the outer limits of what it means
to live as Yahweh's child? How would that change the story?

The blunder theory forgets something Ruth would never forget. She had sworn her allegiance to Naomi. No matter what the
future held for Ruth, she isn't about to turn away from Naomi
and start thinking about herself. Naomi can talk all she likes
about finding rest for Ruth. Ruth already found it the day she
took refuge under Yahweh's wing. It is from this place of rest and
security that Ruth finds the strength and freedom to lay down her
life for Naomi. Submission isn't an act of mindless compliance,
but an act of wisdom, strength, and determination.

Thus, instead of following Naomi's carefully crafted instruc-
tion to wait for Boaz to tell her what to do, Ruth changes course

and commands Boaz. "Spread the corner of your garment over me, since you are a kinsman-redeemer" (Ruth 3:9). In a single sentence she appeals to both the levirate and the kinsman-redeemer laws. It's an unexpected legal twist that actually proves to be brilliant.

Clearly, she is proposing marriage. The action she refers to "probably reflects a marriage custom still attested among Arabs whereby a man symbolically took a wife by throwing a garment-corner over her."[5] The reference to his identity as kinsman-redeemer raises the subject of land. By putting both marriage and land together, Ruth makes clear that her intention is to bear a child to inherit the land she is asking Boaz to redeem.

Considering the fact that Ruth has lost a ten-year battle with barrenness, her proposal is simply astonishing. Boaz sees it right away, which is why his first response is a flood of praise for this radical display of selfless love [*hesed*]. True to her vow, she is making an unprecedented sacrifice to rescue Naomi's family, and Boaz knows it. Ruth is voluntarily sticking out her neck in a dozen different ways and exposing herself to all sorts of potential humiliations. But Ruth never seems to travel on safe roads, and she's walking through a minefield here. She risks his refusal. She risks reopening one of the most painful chapters of her life by trying once more to conceive a child. She risks public embarrassment if anything goes badly and word gets out. Instead of making life better for herself as Naomi desired, Ruth has deliberately put her future in greater jeopardy.

But Ruth has already cast off from shore. Two cords bind her and will still be wrapped firmly around her heart when her body lies silent in the grave. She has tied the knots herself. Heart and soul, Ruth belongs to Yahweh. His *hesed* courses through her veins, and she loves him best by loving and sacrificing for Naomi. And in the boldest act of faith, she steps out and, undaunted by years of barrenness, volunteers to bear a child.

From Ruth's perspective, Naomi's scheme was flawed from the start, for it simply wasn't possible for Ruth to embrace a course of action that put her own happiness ahead of Naomi's. Instead, Ruth sees in Naomi's suggestion a window of opportunity to do more for her mother-in-law than anyone had a right to ask or would even dream. But that, again, is the nature of *hesed*. "Ruth subordinated her own happiness to the family duty of providing Naomi an heir. In demonstrating remarkable initiative and defiance of custom, she not only embodied the Israelite ideal of *hesed* but also, if successful, set herself up to be the true bringer of salvation in this story."[6]

We are watching Ruth pour herself out for Naomi. This is a powerful act of submission. Ruth lays down her life for Naomi and volunteers to conceive a child to rescue the Elimelech family from extinction. She is breaking the rules once again. The words Jesus spoke of another Gentile are surely fitting here. "I tell you the truth, I have not found anyone in Israel with such great faith" (Matthew 8:10). Ruth, out of her poverty, is giving away all she has. Even from the misery and heartache of barrenness, she makes a sacrifice. She offers herself to save Naomi. This is the gospel. This is submission. This is how God's kingdom looks on earth.

BOAZ BREAKS THE RULES

Awakened in the dead of night, from the deep, well-deserved sleep that comes after a long hard day of work and the satisfaction of a job well done, Boaz's life is about to change yet again. The Moabitess is back with a new proposal that will put him into a new conflict of interest and reveal that a man of valor can be powerfully submissive too.

I love the collision moments between this respectable, established man of valor who has spent an entire lifetime meticulously coloring inside the lines and the irrepressible foreigner who for most of her life didn't even know such lines existed. In every encounter she shakes him up, challenges his thinking, and expands his vision of the possibilities for obedience to Yahweh. Here in the darkness, she does it again. Like Lucy of C. S. Lewis' Chronicles of Narnia, Boaz crawls into a stuffy wardrobe of old coats and established traditions carefully preserved in mothballs, only to discover (with a little help from Ruth) an opening in the back and a whole new world of unexplored possibilities beyond.

What is always surprising about Boaz is that he listens and doesn't take offense or become defensive. She's invading his space — first his land and now his life — asking him to change the way he thinks and does things. She turns everything upside down. Yet she isn't manipulating or exploiting Boaz's vulnerability or weakness. She's appealing directly to his strength. And every time she does so in a way that honors him, especially now when under cover of darkness he is free to decide what to do without losing face. Boaz comes through every time. His heart belongs to Yahweh, and so he listens and weighs her words carefully.

Ruth was stretching the gleaning laws when she asked permission to glean behind the harvesters. Now she stretches the levirate and kinsman-redeemer laws to the breaking point. Levirate marriage was a *brother's* responsibility. Boaz is not a brother; he's more likely a cousin. This law doesn't apply to him. What is worse — and certainly embarrassing for Ruth — he isn't the nearest *go'el* either.

On both counts, Boaz has every right to shrug his shoulders and shake his head. "Sorry. This is someone else's problem, not mine." But *hesed* is in Boaz's genes too, and so he doesn't walk away. Ruth may continue walking tightropes, but from this point on there is a safety net below. For the sake of the kinsman who has the first right of refusal, Boaz steps aside. He cannot marry Ruth or redeem Elimelech's property. But if for some reason the kinsman refuses, Boaz pledges himself as Ruth's insurance policy. "Stay here for the night," he tells her, "and in the morning if he wants to redeem, good; let him redeem. But if he is not willing, as surely as the LORD lives I will do it. Lie here until morning" (Ruth 3:13). Boaz will not cover or touch her for the sake of his brother.

The heart of Boaz is aflame — not with testosterone and the anticipation of satisfying his sensual pleasures in the arms of a young woman. His heart is fueled by the same *hesed* and self-sacrificing passion that compelled Naomi to send Ruth to him this night and that drove Ruth to edit Naomi's script. He is his brother's keeper, even a brother long dead. Boaz displays the same love and sacrifice that lives again generations down the road in his descendant, Jesus of Nazareth. As one of my friends says, "You just gotta love Boaz."

We are watching Boaz pour himself out—for Naomi, for Ruth, and for Elimelech. This is a powerful act of submission. He doesn't jump to conclusions, but listens and gives a young widow her voice. The issues she raises are not his responsibility, but before Yahweh, he knows that is irrelevant. And so he pledges—calls God to witness and hold him accountable—to give himself to save the family.

The teachings of Jesus are lived out in this man of valor. "Whoever tries to keep his life will lose it, and whoever loses his life will preserve it" (Luke 17:33). Even though there are enough legal loopholes here to make defense attorneys salivate, Boaz refuses all exit doors and willingly makes a sacrifice. He offers himself and his possessions to help those who are in need. This is the gospel. This is submission. This is how God's kingdom looks on earth.

THE ANCESTORS OF JESUS

I hope I never get over the powerful gospel message that radiated from Bethlehem on that night so long ago. Three ancestors of Jesus, pouring out their lives for one another, sending signals—like three glowing flares in the night sky—that there is a better way to live than the world's way. That we are destined for something more and better than to build the good life for ourselves. We were created to be like Jesus, and we can't be like him if we leave out submission.

Like *hesed*, submission is another of God's great power tools for changing human lives, renovating this fallen planet, and putting our world to rights. It is the point where the kingdom of God powerfully intersects with human culture and begins to transform it from the inside out as those who follow Jesus learn to pour out their lives for others. One wonders how different our world would be—how changed the evening news, how sharply abuse and violence statistics would decline, and how our relationships with one another would be enriched—if God's people truly heeded the call to the kind of submission Jesus advocates and we got serious about looking out for others. This is how Jesus works through us to bring wholeness to our broken world.

FOLLOWING JESUS

Jesus calls his followers to take up their cross and follow him (Mark 8:34–35). Paul collars every believer when he exhorts us to "submit to one another out of reverence for Christ" (Ephesians 5:21). He doesn't leave anyone out. The apostle addresses the whole church when he writes: "Your attitude should be the same as that of Christ Jesus" (Philippians 2:5, NLT). He could hardly have been more pointed.

In dealings with unbelievers, our submission is *redemptive*. We have a world to rescue, and submission is one of God's secret weapons for penetrating behind Enemy lines to recover lost souls. It isn't a hard sell, but a soft approach that targets and woos hearts for Christ. It was the hope of the first-century church that Christian women would win their unbelieving husbands over to faith in Christ by redoubling their efforts to love and submit to them; that through faithful, diligent work believing slaves would lead their masters to kneel before the one true Master over all; that believing children by their honor and obedience would bring their parents to the Father; and that the costly, sacrificial love of husbands, fathers, and masters who are trying to be more like Jesus would improve the lives and soften the hearts of those in their care and draw them to follow him too.

Ultimately the impact of submission means those with power over others give it up. Women grow strong and flourish as kingdom builders. Children thrive and begin to realize their calling to give back. And slaves walk free, side by side in full equality with their Christian brothers who were once their masters.

When dealing with fellow believers, submission aims much higher than simply keeping the peace or resolving stalemates.

A bone-of-my-bone *oneness* is in view, like the oneness Jesus enjoyed with his Father. Not a reluctant, resentful compliance, but a full embrace of a common vision and a mutual delight. Points of difference are opportunities for us to live the gospel, to embody what we believe, to listen, understand, and care, to lay our lives down for one another, to be like Jesus. God created us for this. Eugene Peterson agrees:

> Giving ... is the air into which we were born. It is the action that was designed into us before our birth. Giving is the way the world is. God gives himself. He also gives away everything that is. He makes no exceptions for any of us. We are given away to our families, to our neighbors, to our friends, to our enemies—to the nations. Our life is for others. That is the way creation works. Some of us try desperately to hold on to ourselves, to live for ourselves ... afraid to risk ourselves on the untried wings of giving ... and the longer we wait the less time we have for the soaring and swooping life of grace.[7]

The same radical spirit of submission we see in Jesus shone brightly in Bethlehem the night Naomi sent Ruth to Boaz at the threshing floor. Submission isn't a tiebreaker, a fire extinguisher, a reinforcement of male authority, an act of dutiful compliance, a mindless caving to another's wishes, or a sign of weakness. It is an act of strength, of sober responsibility, and of commitment to God. The voluntary taking up of a cross; the freedom to lay down your life. It is the pursuit of God's glory and the good of another. It is becoming more like Jesus. Submission is the gospel—God's kingdom come on earth.

THE FUTURE INVADES THE PAST

In the name of parental guidance, most parents shield their children's eyes from the Bethlehem threshing floor scene. The adult subjects and sexual content seem inappropriate for young children. Certainly no parent would want their daughter to take a risk like Ruth took. But we are mistaken when we censor scenes like this, for what we have before us is actually a powerful picture of Jesus and his gospel. We are standing on holy ground, for this scene ranks along-side other earthshaking gospel moments in the Old Testament—-like Abraham sacrificing Isaac and Joseph forgiving his brothers. We see Jesus here, and our children need to see him too.

This radical scene also exposes why it's a mistake to think of teaching our daughters to be more compliant or why (for that matter) it's wrong to turn a blind eye when our sons set out in search of wives they can count on to give in when disagreements arise. Dr. Lisa McMinn, a mother of three daughters and a college professor with a keen sensitivity to the challenges facing young women today, offers us a better option—one I think Naomi, Ruth, Boaz, and, yes, also Jesus would approve.

In her book *Growing Strong Daughters*,[8] McMinn advocates raising our daughters to be strong—strong in God, strong thinkers and doers—women committed to Jesus Christ who use their voices to speak truth, who advocate for others, and who join their brothers in living for Jesus at all cost. Raise them to embrace Jesus' brand of submission and to be willing and ready to pour out their lives for his gospel. This is the kingdom of God. Women and men like this become the face of Jesus in our world.

But won't this throw male/female relationships off kilter? When women are strong, aren't they inclined to dominate and men more likely to shrink back into passivity? What happens when women are strong, when they lead out and take the initiative? When women are strong, do men become stronger, or are they weakened?

If you still wonder, after watching interactions between Boaz and Ruth, the next chapter is one you won't want to miss. In the fourth and final scene of the book of Ruth, this predominately female story shifts suddenly into what some perceive as a disappointing return to the world of men. But what happens next can scarcely be called a disappointment. The narrator, who started this story with a surprise beginning, still has a few more surprises in store. And so we leave Ruth and Naomi as they debrief over the night's events and make our way to Bethlehem with Boaz, who will not rest until he settles matters for Ruth and Naomi.

DISCUSSION QUESTIONS

1. How has the concept of submission come up in your life?

2. Why is submission a lifestyle rather than an occasional event?

3. Why does the call to submission apply to men as well as women?

4. How does Jesus change our understanding of submission?

5. How does submission show up in Naomi's life? In Ruth's? In Boaz's?

6. What is the impact on their relationships?

7. How does submission reflect Jesus' gospel and become a powerful force in transforming lives and relationships?

8. Why does Jesus' brand of submission require more of us instead of less?

Chapter Nine

WHEN WOMEN INITIATE
AND MEN RESPOND

"Why it's too pretty a day to be so unhappy."

The inviting voice belonged to a man in his early forties, the unhappiness to a girl the age of twelve. The location is Japan of the 1930s. His words mark the point of intersection in the lives of two total strangers and the collision of two vastly different worlds. As a mother, I feel a chill in my bones when I read the account, for this is exactly the kind of scenario we try to prepare our children to flee. Little Sayuri would have been wise to flee too. Only she had no place to go. Trapped in a culture that rendered her helpless, she is drawn to the kindness of the man who has taken notice of her.

Arthur Golden's best-selling novel, *Memoirs of a Geisha*, chronicles the life of a young Japanese girl sold into slavery by her desperately poor parents—an appalling transaction in human flesh repeated in real life thousands upon thousands of times throughout the world's sordid history and still happening today in shocking numbers. Sayuri is trafficked into the world of the geisha—the upper-class counterpart of the common prostitute. She is destined to become "a butterfly of the night." Her youthful beauty, artistic accomplishments, and virginity will go to the highest bidder from among a coterie of prosperous Japanese businessmen. The Chairman—the elegant man approaching her now—is one of them.

Their first meeting seems innocuous enough. He wipes her tears with his handkerchief and sends her skipping on her way with a coin to buy a shaved ice treat, never to forget his kindness. Like a radiant full moon against the blackened sky, it is a snapshot of glaring contrasts—two human beings dwelling in the same universe, simultaneously inhabiting separate worlds. She is female. Powerless, dependent, vulnerable, voiceless, and (except for the coin he just pressed into her small hand) penniless too. He lives in the privileged world of men and is possessed of power, self-determination, education, and wealth. The disparity between them will never go away and stirs up subliminal questions. What will he do with his advantages? Will he exploit her too? Or is he her ticket to freedom?

Colliding Worlds in Bethlehem

One would never imagine this fictitious encounter to have anything in common with the beautiful story of Ruth. But a similarly chilling meeting between two strangers and a similar clash of worlds takes place in Ruth's story too, with the same ominous possibilities. Ruth's first meeting with Boaz is likewise signaled by the sound of a man's voice. "Whose young woman is that?" the powerful landowner quietly inquires when he sees an unfamiliar gleaner in his field (Ruth 2:5). Like Sayuri, Ruth is trapped in a culture that renders her helpless, although for different reasons. Barrenness, coupled with the deaths of her husband and father-in-law, converted the world into a dangerous place for Ruth and her mother-in-law. They're reduced to a hand-to-mouth subsistence, completely vulnerable to abuse, and written off by the culture as worthless for no other reason than that they are women.

As happens to so many women who hear enough negativity about themselves, Naomi becomes an accomplice in her own depreciation. She accepts the culture's verdict and announces she is "empty." She feels drained of meaning and value. There is nothing left of her, and she has nothing to offer anyone else. This is a living death. Just ask Naomi and she will tell you, "A woman has no life without a man." Even when she reemerges from her debilitating depression, she operates within the boundaries of the culture's value system by seeking for her daughter-in-law what she believes is a woman's only path to meaning and fulfillment. Naomi seeks a husband for Ruth.

On this point, Ruth and her mother-in-law don't see eye to eye. Ruth is convinced she can make a contribution and doesn't intend to let anything stand in her way. She consistently rejects the cultural parameters that confine her sex. Contrary to the culture's rules of widowhood, she uses her wits and her voice without hesitation. She challenges the status quo, offers deeper interpretations of Jewish law, initiates a cogent plan of action, and recruits a man to join her cause. Despite the dangers and the potential for a humiliating rebuff or worse, Ruth has a crucial job to do and a lot is riding on her success in doing it. She lives before the face of Yahweh. *He* defines her, not the culture or her demographics or her despondent mother-in-law, and Ruth doesn't read "empty" in Yahweh's eyes.

The difference between Ruth's story and Sayuri's can be explained in part because of Ruth's unwillingness to concede to the culture or to her circumstances and her fiercely determined activism on Naomi's behalf. But part of the explanation also rests with Boaz, who like the Chairman is a man of unquestionable influence and power in the community. But in every other respect, he is *nothing* like the Chairman. True, in every encounter with Ruth, Boaz is caught in the crosshairs of the same dilemma that confronted the Chairman. How will a man born to advantage regard an unprotected woman, whose sex positions her socially from birth as a weaker vessel? Will he exploit? Or will he empower? Will he use his power to pursue justice and mercy, or become corrupted by indifference, selfish motives, and outright abuse. Yet on every occasion, Boaz reveals he too is Yahweh's child and proves to be as refreshingly unpredictable and full of surprises as his young counterpart from Moab.

Role Reversal in Bethlehem

If you stop to think about it, from the culture's point of view the relationship between Ruth and Boaz is upside down from the start. When she enters his field for the first time, he is clearly the man in charge. Yet she has the nerve to suggest a change in how he's doing things. In round two, at the threshing floor, she and Naomi engineer a plan for marriage and are intent on roping Boaz into pulling it off. No matter how we try to finesse the details to come up with a different scenario, there's simply no getting around the fact that Ruth is the initiator and Boaz is the responder. Suddenly the once quietly stable Bethlehem turns topsy-turvy as women drive the action and a prominent man in the community embraces their ideas and throws his full weight behind their initiatives. It happens that way with Ruth and Boaz every time.

By the final chapter of the story, some might say Boaz has forfeited his power by surrendering it to a foreign gleaner. He is minding his own business (minding it carefully and doing rather well, according to his neighbors), when he is accosted in the night by a woman proposing marriage and leaving him with a truckload of family responsibilities that aren't his worry in the first place.

Yet instead of firmly reminding her of the way things are supposed to work, he's up the next morning before the crack of dawn, shredding his to-do list and notifying his assistant to cancel all engagements for the day. A busy man with a schedule packed full with time-sensitive, end-of-season projects is dropping everything and heading into town on a mission Ruth and her mother-in-law cooked up—two women who also happen to be among the least significant members of Bethlehem society. They are hardly the kind of VIPs for whom a man suspends his business engagements for the day. What is happening to Boaz?

Taking a Closer Look at Ruth and Boaz

Ruth and Boaz take us into complicated areas of relationships between men and women. We normally tiptoe around this aspect of the story and discount Ruth and Boaz as role models because, to be honest, their relationship doesn't fit the way most of us think men and women are supposed to behave toward one another. We try not to think too much about the fact that a woman has proposed marriage to a man and move on to the conclusion of the book. We already know how God means for things to work, and trying to factor their interactions into our thinking pushes us too far. They've already done enough "rule-breaking" without tampering with our understanding of male/female relationships.

Still, they are hard to ignore when the Bible casts them in such a favorable light. That at least opens the possibility that we just might benefit by studying their interactions more closely, even if they do make us uneasy. Like the people who heard and saw Jesus, we are regularly shocked, unsettled, and stretched by what we discover when we probe beneath the surface of God's Word. But we are always better off for working past our preconceived ideas, even our deeply held convictions and our fears, to get to the heart of his message for us. After all, isn't one of the purposes of God's Word to correct us?

So, what happens when a woman takes the initiative and a man responds? Does the earth spin off its axis? Do the foundations of human society as God designed them begin to crumble? What do we stand to lose (or gain) when a man empowers a woman? Is her femininity compromised? Is she usurping a man's role? Does his stature in the community slip? Is his manhood diminished or his self-esteem trampled underfoot? What happens to a man when the tables are turned and he ends up following a woman (or in this case, following two of them)?

REENTRY INTO THE WORLD OF MEN

A rare biblical sojourn into the world of women comes to an end in the final scene of our story as we leave Ruth and Naomi and accompany Boaz to the Bethlehem gate. Here we make an abrupt reentry into the world of men that dominates the ancient culture and most of the Scriptures. Here we'll overhear a group of them deliberating over business matters, and we'll gain more insight into Boaz and discover what he stands to lose by following Ruth.

To be truthful, I have always thought this episode was the least interesting of the book—a bunch of men talking real estate and finance. I'm drumming my fingers, waiting for Boaz to bring up Ruth and for the wedding festivities to begin, eager to move on to the miraculous birth of Obed. Now, however, instead of feeling bored, I'm beginning to think there is more suspense and intrigue here than in all the other chapters combined. Instead of winding down into a dull, predictable ending, the plot grows thicker and the story that started out with a surprise beginning concludes with an explosive finale.

THE CITY GATE

In ancient times, the city gate was not only the point of entry into town and the most logical place to look for fellow villagers coming and going, it was also the heart of the community. The gate was the seat of government and the site of important business transactions, a platform for local dignitaries, a pulpit for prophetic messages, and the hub of local gossip for the entire village. So whenever you hear of someone being praised in the gates (like the legendary woman of Proverbs 31),[1] the entire community from the top down is honoring them. It's comparable to a New York City ticker tape parade for a national hero or having your name emblazoned on a star inlaid on the sidewalk at Hollywood and Vine. Praise in the gates is high honor indeed.

Boaz is heading straight for Bethlehem's gate where he plans to assemble a quorum of city elders to deliberate and rule on legal matters and seal business transactions for the Elimelech family. This is not a closed-door session. Deliberations take place in full view of the curious public as villagers congregate to see what the commotion is all about and to witness the proceedings. Here, along with all Bethlehem, we will discover the enormity of what Boaz is giving up.

Boaz's urgency is matched by the speed with which the relevant parties of his business come together. Almost immediately he spots Elimelech's anonymous nearest relative (scholars nick-named him Mr. No-Name) and calls him aside. Before you know it, Boaz has collected ten Bethlehem elders, and an ad hoc meeting of the ancient court is gaveled into session. A jury of ten men will decide Ruth's fate. What happens next leaves modern readers scratching their heads, as legal codes and local customs entirely foreign to us play out, and Boaz with the savvy and surprise of a well-prepared district attorney makes his case.

BOAZ GOES TO BAT

Right away, Boaz catches readers off-guard by raising the subject of land, when we are expecting him to present the more pressing matter (at least from our vantage point) of who will marry Ruth. For some unknown reason, Boaz changes the first order of business from marriage to real estate. We have forgotten that Ruth already raised the subject of Elimelech's property, for when she appealed to Boaz as the family's kinsman-redeemer, she targeted his responsibility to buy and reactivate Elimelech's abandoned fields.[2]

While we may find Boaz's tactics confusing, he knows exactly what he's doing. He is speaking a language these men understand, for the most tantalizing part of the bargain he is putting in front of his relative isn't Ruth, but the piece of land once cultivated by Elimelech that now lies fallow. Under Mosaic legal code, the Promised Land belonged to Yahweh but was subdivided and parceled out permanently by tribe and family. Each man took possession of his own land. In an agrarian culture, a man's land is the family business and the centerpiece of the inheritance he passes on to his sons. Elimelech's land must be redeemed, and the relative who takes home the deed will probably be doubling his own estate.

When a hurricane blasts through Florida (which happens frequently), homeowners patch up holes in their own roofs and clear away fallen trees and debris from their own yards before helping out a neighbor. According to law, Mr. No-Name was first in line to assist Elimelech in recovering his land during hard times.

But just like a hurricane, the unforgettable and seemingly endless Bethlehem famine hit everyone with hard times all at once. Everybody was coping with dried up fields, crop failures, and food shortages. Consumed by the needs of their own families, Mr. No-Name, Boaz, and the other men in the region were in no position to help out Elimelech or anyone else. Now that the famine is finally over and the countryside is in recovery mode, they're in a better position to discuss land issues again.

What is also surprising about Boaz's first order of business, however, is the fact that he describes this abandoned piece of property as *Naomi's* land. When did widows start inheriting their husband's property, scholars want to know? Mosaic Law made an exception so *daughters* could inherit land in families without sons, but only if they married within their father's clan, for the whole objective of the law was to keep a man's land within his tribe.[3] If a man had neither sons nor daughters, then his land went to his brothers and, in lieu of brothers, to his nearest relative. Nowhere are widows given rights of inheritance. And it is one of the most frightening injustices in the world today, that widows are evicted from their husband's land and left to fend for themselves and their children on the streets.

The only way a widow could hang on to her husband's property and protect it from seizure by her husband's relatives was if she had an heir or could produce one. On both counts, Naomi was out of luck. Already Boaz seems to be breaking the rules by granting Naomi rights to Elimelech's land. Surprisingly, no one seems to object to this or any of the other terms Boaz adds to these arrangements.

Perhaps this is as good a place as any to remind ourselves of how the narrator originally introduced Boaz—as a man of valor and high standing in the community. We assumed this description was purely a recommendation for his suitability as a prospective husband for Ruth. But these admirable qualities also set us up for the scene at the Bethlehem gate and help us understand the substantial clout Boaz clearly possesses in these legal proceedings and why he is able to press forward with Ruth's initiatives without the slightest protest from the other men.

It is entirely possible that Boaz isn't the sort of man anyone would want to oppose. This imposing man has earned a place of stature in the community because of his character and his achievements, which by themselves explain the kind of influence he wields in these deliberations. Not until the conclusion of the narrative do we learn that Boaz's stature in the community is also genetic. The genealogy that concludes the book of Ruth identifies Boaz as an Israelite blueblood—the direct descendant of Nahshon, one of Israel's greatest leaders. During the time of Moses, Boaz's grandfather,[4] Nahshon, was the tribal chief of Judah, Israel's largest tribe, and the commanding general of the largest division of the Israelite army. When the cloud of God's glory lifted and the Israelites broke camp, Nahshon led the tribe of Judah out first.[5] At the dedication of the tabernacle, Nahshon was the first tribal chief to offer sacrifices.[6] Anyone born in this family was something of a Kennedy in the ancient culture—a member of the nation's first family—an identity that brought with it a natural expectation of high-profile leadership in the community.

Putting all of this together, Naomi and Ruth couldn't have found a more powerful advocate than Boaz. His advocacy for them carries enormous weight and forms a solid barrier against the inevitable exploitations widows often suffered. Boaz is a leader among leaders and wields his advantages in wise and righteous ways that promote *hesed* within the community. Consequently, Bethlehem elders don't raise the slightest objection to the notion of Naomi selling land, but follow Boaz's lead in making allowances. This is only the beginning.

READY TO STRIKE A BARGAIN

Mr. No-Name is, of course, impacted by this unexpected development, for he is the rightful heir to Elimelech's land and stands to inherit by default without doing anything at all. This inevitable and natural transfer of ownership is threatened by Boaz, however, who applies not-too-subtle pressure on his relative to act now, by stating his intention to purchase Naomi's land if Mr. No-Name declines.

You can almost see the wheels turning in the primary kins-man-redeemer's head. Admittedly, the slight complication of hav-ing to consider Naomi is a bit odd, but it is minor compared to what he stands to gain if he secures Elimelech's property for himself. Waiting to take possession until Naomi's death is a small price to pay for the eventual increase in his personal estate.

Buying the land from Naomi now and investing his personal resources to get things in working order will only mean the land is already turning a profit when his family takes possession at her death. Even if it costs him a sizeable chunk of money now, a little tightening of his financial belt for the present is a smarter move than ceding the land to Boaz. In the absence of an Elimelech family heir, this is a no-lose proposition and a lucrative deal. No man in his right mind would turn it down. Mr. No-Name eagerly pulls out his pen and prepares to sign on the dotted line.

OUT OF LEFT FIELD

Up to this point in proceedings, Boaz hasn't mentioned Ruth. For all intents and purposes, she is irrelevant to this discussion and might as well be invisible. Boaz is about to change all that. In a brilliant move that no one sees coming, he brings Ruth in as part of the bargain and the linchpin for the entire transac-tion. "On the day you acquire the field from Naomi, you acquire Ruth the Moabitess, the wife of the deceased, in order to raise up descendants for the deceased on his inheritance" (Ruth 4:5, Bush translation).

Most of us assume that the added condition of marriage to Ruth was no surprise to Naomi's relatives, that they all saw it coming. But if Mr. No-Name's reaction is any indicator, it was wholly unexpected, for he immediately backs out of the deal. It is important to point this out, for one of the puzzles in the book of Ruth is why the men in the story seem slow to address a family in crisis.

Popular Bible studies on the book of Ruth may not reflect this, but in scholarly discussions the men of Bethlehem actually come under a lot of criticism for failing to act sooner. The nearest relative seems negligent in fulfilling his familial duties to Elimelech. Boaz (who supposedly has his heart set on Ruth) is inexplicably slow in making his move to secure her as his bride. He deserves a lot of credit for granting her special gleaning privileges, but even there he might have done more. If he really was as captivated by Ruth as many believe, why didn't he send her home with the promise that from now on his servants will be making regular stops by the house with plenty of food to take care of them? Isn't that what any true lover would do?

In addition to the shortcomings of Boaz and Mr. No-Name, the leaders of the community fail to hold Elimelech's relatives accountable to fulfill their duty. There is plenty of blame to go around. It is hard to justify how the men of Bethlehem could carry on with business as usual when, by neglecting their obligations to Elimelech, his widow and daughter-in-law are suffering hardship and living as paupers, not to mention the disturbing fact that Elimelech's name is being wiped from the memory of the community.

Caring for Ruth and Naomi's physical needs is one thing, and the men of Elimelech's family are culpable for not doing more. Marriage to Ruth, however, is an entirely different matter. It extends well beyond the call of duty and the scope of the law, and none of the men can be faulted here. When Boaz brings up Ruth, a lot of missing pieces begin to come together and what should have been a routine purchase of land becomes a high-stakes gamble.

A DEAL-BREAKER

In the eyes of the culture and of the men in Elimelech's family, *Naomi* is "the widow of the deceased." The property under discussion belonged to *Naomi's* husband, Elimelech. The levirate law applied to *Naomi*, Elimelech's childless widow, but is now no longer relevant since she is past childbearing age. This was how Naomi saw things too, for she spells it out in the starkest of terms when she speaks to Orpah and Ruth. "I am too old to have another husband. Even if I thought there was still hope for me—even if I had a husband tonight and then gave birth to sons—would you wait until they grew up?" (Ruth 1:12–13).

Ruth's proposal of marriage to Boaz was another example of her unsettling habit of looking beyond the letter of the law to pursue its spirit. The letter of the law required a childless man's *brother* to marry and impregnate his widow. In this situation, Boaz and Mr. No-Name could walk away with a clear conscience, for they were not Elimelech's brother, and Naomi would never get pregnant. The spirit of the law, however, said, "Save the family," which binds the hearts of Yahweh's children and moves them to find a way to do the impossible.

Ruth accepted responsibility to save the family and figured out a way to help Naomi navigate around this impassible roadblock. She volunteers herself to bear a child for the family in Naomi's place and calls on Boaz to step in for Elimelech's nonexistent brother. The child produced from the union between Ruth and one of Elimelech's kinsman-redeemers will be Elimelech's heir on town records and will inherit his land. This was the second time she confronted Boaz with a radical proposal. And for the second time, he catches the significance of what she's doing and becomes a willing ally for her radical cause.

The idea is highly irregular and probably without precedent. What makes it a high-stakes gamble is the fact that Ruth is barren and has been for years. There's a good chance she may never conceive. If Mr. No-Name marries her and she remains childless, the land becomes his free and clear. He has enriched himself and his heirs, and everything he has invested in Naomi's land goes back into his own pocket. Then again, considering how Yahweh is already shaking things up in Bethlehem through the young Moabitess, there's no telling what might happen. "Is anything too hard for the LORD?" (Genesis 18:14). The nearest kinsman-redeemer can't take that chance.

Mr. No-Name's decision to relinquish his rights exposes the enormity of the sacrifice that Boaz is willing to make. In this scene, the nearer kinsman-redeemer serves the same purpose for Boaz that Orpah served for Ruth when her sensible choice to return to Moab set in sharp relief the radical nature of Ruth's choice to remain with Naomi. The narrator doesn't demonize Orpah or Mr. No-Name as self-centered or evil. Both make culturally acceptable responses to an extremely difficult choice. Whoever redeems Naomi's land must siphon off resources from his own estate to purchase and then rehabilitate Elimelech's overgrown fields. If Ruth gives birth, the kinsman-redeemer who fathers her child faces financial ruin because everything he's invested, along with Elimelech's estate, will go to her child. As a result, he will leave to his own sons a fraction of what he would pass on by simply keeping things as they are.

Mr. No-Name follows good decision-making logic by assessing the odds and deciding marriage to Ruth is too big of a gamble. Like Orpah, Mr. No-Name is sensible and does what anyone would expect under the circumstances. He does not do *hesed* to his relative Elimelech. To Boaz he replies, "I cannot redeem [Elimelech's land] because I might endanger my own estate. You redeem it yourself. I cannot do it" (Ruth 4:6). Ironically, the man who seeks to preserve his inheritance loses his own name in the process. No one remembers the real name of Mr. No-Name, who passes over to Boaz the right to redeem Elimelech's land. To document this transfer, the nearer kinsman follows ancient custom by removing his sandal and handing it over to Boaz.[7]

A RESCUE OPERATION

In Cinderella stories, this is the moment when the glass slipper fits. The fairy godmother appears out of nowhere to transform the shabby cinder girl into the beautiful princess—complete with ball gown and tiara—and the prince rescues her from a life of hardship and drudgery and carries her off in a golden carriage to a happily-ever-after future.

If we buy into that explanation here, we do a terrible disservice to Boaz as well as to Ruth, and we lose the power of the gospel that this narrative so richly conveys. The story becomes all about what Ruth and Boaz are *getting*, instead of what they are giving up. Boaz becomes the kinsman-redeemer hero who follows his heart to rescue Ruth and make her life fulfilling and complete with marriage and a baby. And we set ourselves up for frustration because we are left with a story that bears no resemblance to the real world where we live and remains perpetually out of reach for us when our own happily-ever-after fairy tale doesn't come true.

Only moments ago, Mr. No-Name gulped when he read the staggering price tag on marriage to Ruth. He refused to redeem his brother because the potential cost was wildly out of his price range. He fears it will ruin him, and he is right. Faced with yet another conflict of interest posed by Ruth, the nearer kinsman-redeemer chooses to look out for himself. In sharp contrast (and the narrator means for us to make this comparison and to be shocked by it), Boaz moves forward with fearless determination to the marriage altar. He displays the same radical, risk-it-all brand of self-sacrifice that we have repeatedly observed in Ruth. This is the gospel. Boaz is doing *hesed*, and in this he is Ruth's match.

A rescue operation is underway in Bethlehem. But it is *not* to rescue Ruth, as is often supposed. Elimelech is the one in trouble and in need of a kinsman-redeemer. No one knows exactly what went wrong. Maybe he was simply down on his luck and the famine pushed him over the edge. Desperate to protect his family from starvation, he packed them up and migrated to Moab in an evacuation plan that ultimately backfired. Maybe the explanation was just that simple. Or maybe he was the black sheep of the family, the renegade who took off for Moab to save his own skin instead of sticking together with everyone else. The fact is no one really knows.

What we do know is that hope for Elimelech's legacy ran out when Naomi buried their sons and her monthly cycles ceased. In the eyes of the community, Elimelech is a lost cause. But Ruth is not ready to concede defeat. In an act of raw courage, she persuades Boaz to join forces with her in rescuing *Elimelech* from the jaws of annihilation and Naomi from the grip of poverty and futility. It is a long shot, and both of them know it. But God specializes in lost causes, and they are both willing to take enormous risks, believing Yahweh is moving them to act and will grant them success.

Yes, Ruth initiates and Boaz responds. There's little doubt of this. But we are seriously mistaken to label this a victory for women and a defeat for men. That's how the world views male/female relationships. But in God's kingdom, those categories simply don't exist, and the Bible isn't interested in that kind of scorecard anyway. This antipatriarchal chapter of biblical history has a deeper message for us than simply another round in the battle of the sexes. It lifts us out of this old debate to look at relationships between men and women from the perspective of God's original vision for us.

Ruth and Boaz have mobilized for a rescue. Someone is in trouble, and they are determined to help. When the "someone" in trouble was my brother-in-law on Mt. Hood, no one in my family cared who initiated a plan of action or who carried it out. It didn't matter to us who led and who followed. We just desperately wanted Kelly and his two friends back safe and sound. Anyone who could help make that happen had our full support, our heartfelt gratitude, our earnest prayers for success.

When Ruth and Boaz launched their small-scale rescue operation, they had no idea that they were reconnecting with God's original vision for his creation. Nor did they ever realize that their local rescue effort was actually crucial to God's global rescue operation to save the lost and self-destructing planet that he loves.

In Bethlehem, God's image bearers—Ruth and Boaz—were ruling and subduing the small portion of earth God entrusted to their stewardship. But even bigger things were happening, for they were rescuing the royal line of the Messiah. The miracle child they both risk everything to conceive becomes the grandfather of King David, the forefather of King Jesus. And through their efforts God is even reactivating Naomi to assume a major role in God's redemptive purposes for the world.

God calls his image bearers to join him in saving the world. This isn't the language of comic books or cartoon heroes, but the central message of the Bible. And in the book of Ruth, *three* of God's image bearers join this battle—led by an *ezer*, to be sure, but this is not a women's movement. This is the Blessed

Alliance—one of the strongest examples we see in the entire Old Testament of God's image bearers—male and female—serving God together. Each of them has a major contribution to make, and the entire cause will suffer severely and the other two will be seriously hampered in their own call to obedience, if one of them backs away.

An Uncommon Union

In this cruel world, even a geisha has more value than the combined worth of two childless widows in a patriarchal culture. Sayuri is desired by men. She is useful for their pleasure. But she has no value in herself. No one hears her thoughts, much less encourages her to think. She has no sense of mission in this world other than to please the men who hold her hostage. She needs rescuing herself and has no thought of rescuing someone else.

Sayuri is drawn by a deep longing to be near the Chairman in hopes of filling the empty void she feels inside. Eventually she becomes the Chairman's geisha—a tragic capitulation to a fallen culture that should fill us with outrage. She remains powerless, dependent, vulnerable, and voiceless, despite her luxurious lifestyle—a beautiful bird in a gilded cage. She never learns to fly.

Ruth's story could have turned out in a similar way. She was just as vulnerable as Sayuri—disadvantaged and defenseless against the superior power of men. And there were men in Bethlehem who would not have hesitated to take advantage of her vulnerability for their own pleasure. When she "happens" into the field of Boaz, Ruth's life begins to change for the better—not because she finally has a man in her sights and is longing to be near him so he can fill the void she feels inside, but because he becomes her advocate—a staunch ally for the vital mission God has given her. Instead of stifling Ruth by insisting that things stay the way they are and making sure he maintains his superior rank and leadership over her, Boaz becomes the wind beneath her wings.

He doesn't simply *permit* what she proposes. He embraces God's call on her life and *promotes* her efforts, at increasingly greater cost to himself. Together they are caught up in a purpose that is bigger than the both of them, but that is what frees them to do what must be done—even if it means breaking the rules in the eyes of the culture. They are pursuing the spirit of God's law, and Yahweh's smile rests upon this Blessed Alliance. The power of the gospel is at work. They are changing the world, and as they serve God together, he is changing them.

Before we conclude our study of Ruth, we have some unfinished business, for the questions we raised in the beginning remain to be answered. So, for Naomi's sake and for our own, let us ask again, Is God good for women?

DISCUSSION QUESTIONS

1. Describe a relationship in your life where you hold the advantage over someone else because of your age, your race, your role or job, your education, status, social or economic class, etc.

2. How does Boaz naturally hold the advantage over Naomi and Ruth?

3. How do Naomi and Ruth initiate their plan?

4. How does Boaz respond and why does his relationship with Ruth break the rules?

5. What did Boaz stand to lose?

6. How does Mr. No-Name help us understand the risks to Boaz and how much he actually gains?

7. How are Boaz and Ruth guided in their actions by their relationship to Yahweh?

8. How are Boaz and Ruth role models for how men and woman are supposed to serve God together?

Chapter Ten

GOOD TO GREAT

"We've decided to err on the side of caution."

The conference was filled with hundreds of women of all ages and walks of life whose souls had been deeply stirred by God's call on their lives and by the staggering needs of a fallen, hurting world. They were captured by God's great cosmic vision, sobered by a deep sense of personal responsibility, and ready to join Jesus' rescue operation with every fiber of their being. But in the closing admonition, instead of being urged to go forward, they were being cautioned to hold back. It felt like someone had sucked all the oxygen out of the room. The rationale? They are women, after all, and need to let the men take the lead. It is the godly thing to do. "Now don't go home or back to your churches with a bunch of big ideas and put pressure on the men."

One woman chose not to heed that counsel. A breast cancer survivor, this single mom had escaped with her children from an abusive marriage. She knew the meaning of isolation and depression. Keenly aware of the kinds of trouble and heartache that go on behind closed doors, she could see familiar signs of desperation in the women at her church and in the surrounding community. She felt responsible to do something. She chose *not* to err on the side of caution and presented to the elders of her church a thoughtful proposal for a ministry she wanted to start for women in crisis. Instead of clearing a path for her to move forward and putting their support behind her (as Boaz did for Ruth), they erred on the side of caution. Their reason for rejecting her proposal was their fear that, in a ministry of such a sensitive nature, "women will gossip."

If Ruth had embraced a philosophy of caution, the negative repercussions would have been devastating and widespread. She almost certainly would have returned to Moab with "cautious" Orpah. Naomi would be a statistic in the headcount of the world's displaced and impoverished widows. She'd have tales to tell about being pushed around, exploited, and mistreated—painful injustices to reinforce her belief that she was worthless and God had turned his back on her. Depressed, isolated, and defeated, the older widow would eventually disappear from sight—withdrawn from the pages of Scripture and swallowed up by irrelevance in the goings on of Bethlehem.

Boaz would have continued basking in the glories of his past achievements while "cautiously" permitting gleaners in his field. His workers would have kept on scraping his fields bare, and he would still be guarding his piles of grain at the threshing floor. The names of Elimelech, Mahlon, and Kilion would be missing from the annuls of Israel's history, erased by their untimely deaths. A "cautious" Mr. No-Name would be rubbing his hands together with glee over the increase in his estate, without giving a thought to Elimelech's destitute widow. A different branch of Judah's family tree would become Israel's royal family and enjoy the distinct honor of producing the Messiah, for God will not be stopped by cautious image bearers. Instead of shining brightly, the gospel would remain hidden in Bethlehem during the dark days when the judges ruled. And we would still be wondering if God is good for women.

THE POWER OF A WOMAN'S COURAGE

But Ruth didn't embrace a philosophy of caution—certainly not where Yahweh's call on her life was concerned. Sometimes following God means throwing caution to the wind. Sometimes caution is a symptom of faithlessness. Instead of quietly blending into her new surroundings (something you'd expect any newcomer to do), she stood out even before she set foot on Jewish soil. Whenever her heart locked on a course of action that was true to her calling as Yahweh's child and beneficial to Naomi, the young Moabitess turned fearless. She stubbornly refused to live as though every new intersection of her life was flashing an amber light at her.

So in place of the dull and disappointing story that we might have gotten — where women accept the culture's verdict on them and wait passively for some dashing man to come to their rescue — we have a power-packed drama of a courageous young heroine who initiates the rescue herself and revolutionizes a man's life by inviting him to join her. Like Jesus, Ruth is new wine poured into Israel's old wineskins. Those old wineskins simply burst under the expanding pressure of her relentless pursuit of the deeper meaning of God's law and her search for more radical ways of loving him.

Ruth is a breath of fresh air in a world where "good" is good enough and God's people settle for small visions of themselves and what God will do through them. Her courageous actions send seismic tremors rippling through ancient Bethlehem. In every episode, she is making sacrifices and shining the bright light of the gospel into the darkened era when the judges ruled. The results are transformational.

Naomi's broken-down life is recharged. Boaz awakens to an expanded vista of how much more a man can (and should) do for others with the undeserved advantages and blessings God has given him. He and Ruth forge an alliance that gives us a rare Old Testament glimpse of the Blessed Alliance, as male and female partner in a holy cause, and both thrive as Yahweh's image bearers. The ancient culture's cruel injustices toward at least one widow are stopped. A family is saved. *Hesed* spreads like wildfire, from the Bethlehem highway through the fields of Boaz and the threshing floor, past the city gates, and into the small veins of a newborn baby boy.

God's fingerprints are on every page of this story as his daughters accept responsibility and do whatever it takes to rule and subdue the portion of earth he has entrusted to them. God's promised future kingdom brushes up against the kingdom of this world. The gospel breaks through, and we get an alluring sneak preview of the way things were meant to be—and will be one day through Jesus. In the midst of all the action, God is speaking to his daughters about the questions that are troubling them. *Everyone* wins when courage fills a woman's soul.

THE GRAND FINALE

In the end, the whole town erupts in celebration as Boaz grasps his kinsman's sandal and announces his determination to fulfill his obligations as Elimelech's kinsman-redeemer. It is a new day in Bethlehem. City elders and villagers, rightly moved by the extraordinary scene they have just witnessed, joyfully surround their native son and bless him with prayers that his name may become famous in their clan and in Bethlehem and that Ruth will bless him with lots of children.

Their prayers for blessing do not exclude the Moabitess, who, although she is physically absent from the scene, nevertheless maintains a strong presence in everyone's mind. In another powerful gospel moment when a Gentile woman is fully embraced, Bethlehemites scoop the young foreigner into the family circle. This happens even before anyone knows whether or not Yahweh will bless the union between Boaz and Ruth with offspring. Villagers link Ruth to some of the brightest female luminaries in Israel's constellation. In the perfect wedding toast, villagers pray that Boaz's wife will become like Leah and Rachel who "built up the house of Israel" (Ruth 4:11). These two sisters (with the help of their two maidservants) presented their husband Jacob with a dozen strapping sons and put the nation on the solid foundation of twelve strong tribes. Bethlehemites pray that, like Rachel and Leah, Ruth will be a nation builder too.

More significantly, they connect Ruth to Tamar,[1] the revered mother of their tribe. She and Ruth have a lot in common. Both were foreigners who married Israelite men. Both are widowed (Tamar twice) and exhibit deep familial loyalty by courageously breaking with social protocol (an understatement in Tamar's case) to rescue their deceased husbands from extinction. As with Ruth, Tamar's righteous actions had a profound spiritual impact on a man. She pulled her father-in-law, Judah, out of a spiritual ditch and back on the solid path, where he thereafter lived as a true son of Yahweh.

Tamar was the mother of Perez, from whom Elimelech, Boaz, Mr. No-Name, and other Bethlehemites descended. Villagers pray that, like Tamar, Ruth will produce a family of greatness that measures up to Perez's family. Yahweh does more than they ask. The genealogy tacked on at the end of her story reveals that Ruth's family surpasses the glories of Perez. Her child Obed (who is three-fourths Gentile[2]) will build the royal house of King David and ultimately produce the long-awaited Messiah.

It is quite a leap for a Moabite outsider, a poor widow, and a common gleaner to be associated with three prominent women from Israel's past. It is an appropriate association and one that sticks, for Ruth becomes permanently enrolled on the roster of Israel's kingdom builders.[3] There is much that can be mined from the inclusion of these strong women in Ruth's story. But at the very least these associations reveal that the community's high opinion of Ruth—as a woman of valor—has not suffered in the slightest by her bold initiatives with Boaz. Instead, they honor her even more.

From this point, the narrator accelerates the action. In a single verse, the long-anticipated wedding between Boaz and Ruth takes place behind the scenes, and we are informed that Yahweh intervenes to reverse Ruth's barrenness. Sometime later—probably within the year—he blesses their union with the birth of a son.

The story concludes with one final snapshot of Naomi sitting contentedly with the newborn Obed in her arms, as the women of the village (presumably some of the same ones who registered shock when she first returned to Bethlehem) gather around to celebrate the birth of Obed and Naomi's good fortune.

Once again, we've reached a juncture in the narrative where it's easy to lose our way. Suddenly, the inspiring story of a young widow's remarkable courage and the gripping saga of an older female Job's agonized wrestlings with Yahweh shift into a lower gear and we notice a serious drop in momentum.

SECOND THOUGHTS

Years ago, I knew I wanted to write a book about Ruth. I've spent hours and hours studying, thinking, asking questions, and processing these four little chapters of the Old Testament. I'm not still reading commentaries at the dinner table, but the book of Ruth is never very far from my thoughts. At times, I've even thought that if someone poked me with a needle, I would bleed the book of Ruth.

This brief narrative—the stories of Ruth and Naomi—has meant more to me and made a bigger difference in my own life than any other study I've ever done. Until I encountered Ruth on the pages of the commentaries of Robert Hubbard, Edward Campbell, Katharine Doob Sakenfeld, Frederic Bush, and several other scholars, I never imagined God had such big callings for women. This alone has changed my vision for myself and for other women. These women taught me that it didn't matter how my life changed or what new bend in the road lay ahead, God always has important kingdom work for me to step out and do. Ruth's story helped me see that neither I nor any of God's daughters belong on the sidelines, while our brothers build his kingdom without us. He means for us to work alongside our brothers, and he is doing *great* things through his daughters, even though we, like Ruth and Naomi, may never live to see the full significance of our contributions.

These scholars also made me realize that God takes women — takes me—seriously. I never imagined such a thing as a female Job existed; that a book of the Bible was devoted to the kinds of struggles, disappointments, and losses women face; or that God is so intensely interested in the cry of a woman's heart. But here she is, this female Job, right on the pages of my Bible—crying out to God, and God is moving heaven and earth (and most especially Ruth and Boaz) to let Naomi know she is not forgotten, not unloved, not meaningless or purposeless.

And now that I'm coming to the end of this book, I'm finding it next to impossible to finish. I keep hitting the brakes. Part of the reason is the fact that I'm always writing in the real world. Whenever I write, I can't shut out the interruptions or the awful background noise I keep hearing. It isn't simply that I see a lot of pain in other people's lives or that friends and loved ones are constantly talking about the hard stuff they're going through. That happens, of course. But, to be honest, I feel a lot of pain myself. This manuscript coincided with the devastating death of my brother-in-law, and the pain and grief over losing him is still very raw in my family. This creates major problems for me when I'm coming down the home stretch and am seeing that, instead of a strong glorious finish that helps us live with hope in our brokenness, the conclusion is disappointing and weak. It simply won't hold up under the pressures of the real world.

The Hebrew writer designed the beginning and the ending of the Ruth story as a chiasm. In simple terms, this means the beginning and the ending of the story are sort of like bookends. A subject that comes up in the beginning comes up again in the end. So in Ruth, for example, what unraveled in the beginning gets put back together in the end. In the beginning Naomi and Ruth are unplugged from their culture. In the end, they are reconnected. In the beginning they lose their husbands and are bereft of children. In the end, there's a man in the family and a baby in their arms. In the beginning Naomi is empty. In the end, her emptiness is filled. In the beginning we hear her God-forsaken cry and in the end everyone is celebrating God's good blessings on Naomi's life.

I see the joy and marvel at the great things God has done for Naomi and for Ruth. But I cannot swallow the typical explanations for why these changes occur. It feels hollow and Disneyesque to me. And the background noise in my life forces me to resist sticking a happily-ever-after banner over the ending. The Bible doesn't teach us that God is working from some divine balance sheet and will eventually even up accounts so that we recover our losses and our sacrifices are repaid.

It's obvious to anyone who has experienced a significant loss that the sorrows of this world and the wounds they inflict in our souls *cannot* be compensated no matter how much good fortune and prosperity come our way. Many holocaust survivors ended up wealthy, raised beautiful families, and enjoyed the good things in life. But they never stopped hurting or felt their sufferings had evened out. That's just not how life works. To suggest that everything balanced out in the end for Naomi is to trivialize both her sufferings and also what God is trying to teach us through her story. I even think it trivializes the men.

I also am deeply troubled that—after seeing the book of Ruth as a powerful Old Testament statement of the gospel and an eye-opening preview of the new world order Jesus is bringing—the ending seems to capitulate to human culture by presenting men as solutions to women's problems, dividing men and women into separate worlds, and installing a male shelter for the fairer sex so women won't have to deal with the crying needs of this broken world or get their hands dirty doing the hard work of ruling and subduing the earth for God's kingdom. Men can handle the hard jobs. All a woman really needs is a man, a baby, and a home to tend, and she'll be happy. Naomi and Ruth find their true place in this world by returning to the domestic sphere, with a man to protect, provide for, and take care of them. Women don't belong in the barley field.

In the ending, Ruth marries and has a baby. Naomi (according to some) is just thrilled to be a grandmother and to be part of a family again. Boaz will take care of everyone, and when he's too old to do the job or dies and widows Ruth a second time, Obed will take over. It's a nice theory. But most women's stories don't end up like that. I can't talk myself into buying the philosophy this promotes. I certainly can't imagine trying to sell it to anyone else. I agree with the commentator who remarked, "What a weak, purposeless ending such a resort to sentimentality gives the otherwise well-told tale."[4] Katherine Sakenfeld elaborates:

> A story with such promising beginnings, as women seek to make their own way, ends very conventionally (albeit through unconventional behavior along the way) with the women's security

achieved by reintegrating themselves completely into the existing traditional economic and family structure. And it is the men who arrange the details of the reintegration.... How can we get beyond the "husband, wife, two children, one dog, one cat" version of "happily ever after"?[5]

For generations this Cinderella interpretation has clouded the church's understanding of the book of Ruth and drained the power out of its message. We are left with a weak conclusion that is full of flaws and that doesn't relate honestly to the realities of our lives. God is inadvertently shoved to the margins. Weddings and babies dominate the discussion. Little wonder the book of Ruth gets classed as a theological lightweight, suitable for mindless bedtime reading. The book itself is in grave danger of becoming irrelevant. I'm convinced we have more digging to do.

To get us back on track, we must restore God to his rightful place as the true hero of the story. If we lose sight of him or allow some other hero or heroine to displace him, we'll miss the whole point of the book. We also need to keep reminding ourselves that we are delving into a culture that is completely foreign to us. Even our concepts of marriage and family are significantly different from those of the patriarchal world, especially where kinsman-redeemer and levirate practices come into play. Boaz and Ruth aren't "starting a family" in the typical way we think of today. They are *rescuing* a family. There's a big difference.

Additionally, we must not let go of the fact that this book is seamlessly woven together from start to finish. It doesn't come unhinged at the last. Earlier themes we identified—Naomi's sufferings, Ruth's radical sacrifices, Boaz's advocacy, and God's large vision for his daughters—all spill into the final scene and run right up to the end. For that matter, the entire Bible itself is a unified whole, so we can't expect this small book to teach that it's okay for women to retire from their *ezer*-warrior callings or withdraw from active membership in the Blessed Alliance.

So looking back over the entire book, what can we conclude?

GOD AND HIS DAUGHTERS

Throwing out a baby girl to die on the dung heap or burning a widow on her husband's funeral pyre are among some of the most appalling value statements the world has ever made about women. Negative statements about women run from these extreme atrocities to milder, more polite forms. But they all belong to the same fallen value system. The Bible's view of women rejects that entire system and introduces a whole new way of thinking. God's views of his daughters and his large vision for their roles in his kingdom are on a collision course with the world's view of women, and that collision is showcased in the book of Ruth.

In a way, the Ruth story reminds me of the prophet Elijah, who poured gallons of water on an altar he actually wanted God to ignite. To make sure no one missed the point of what God was doing, Elijah stacked the deck, so to speak, before he started to pray. The book of Ruth achieves a similar effect by juxtaposing God's view of women against the harshest possible backdrop.

The story begins by taking us into the patriarchal culture—a world that advantages men by birth and automatically sends women to the back of the bus. But reducing women to second-class citizens isn't nearly a dark enough setting for God to make his point. The situation gets much worse.

The two women God selects as Exhibits A and B are thrown off the bus. A series of tragedies, deaths, and disappointments evict Naomi and Ruth from hearth and home—the one sphere a woman could count on for safety and purpose. No longer wives or mothers, they are cast out on their own, stranded in a culture that works against them, deprived of tools, resources, and opportunities they need to get back on their feet. Ground zero is their home address.

Although the ancient Israelite culture didn't burn widows alive, it was still a brutal environment for the disconnected woman. Widows were discarded as though they didn't exist. Had these two widows lived in a culture that observed *sati*, both women would have perished in the flames. Instead, they lived as outcasts in circumstances far worse than *sati* according to a Vrindavan widow who knew what she was talking about.

Against this blackened canvas, God splashes the vivid colors of a totally different view of women. Instead of losing interest in these two useless widows, he makes them the center of attention. Instead of erasing them from his story as noncontributors, he colors them into mission-critical roles. These were the dark days when the judges governed. God's chosen people were losing their way. God's strategy involves recruiting two women to carry his redemptive purposes forward into the future. Ruth and Naomi do not let him down. With all of the heady things that were going on at the time — in palace throne rooms, at city gates, and on international battlefields — Ruth and Naomi capture the headlines.

These women are Yahweh's image bearers. Even their ordinary activities are laden with significance. They represent his interests in this world and a lot is riding on what they do at this crucial juncture in Israel's history. What looks from their vantage point as simple acts of loving and caring for one another will actually take on cosmic proportions. They labor and sacrifice to bring blessing to each other, and simultaneously bring blessing to the world.

As a quick aside, it's worth noting that God did not raise up women because there was a shortage of capable men — an explanation we often hear that's intended to qualify what God is doing through women. But that doesn't apply here. Bethlehem is not suffering from a vacuum of male leadership. To the contrary, Bethlehem boasts at least one man (and probably more) who *epitomized* everything you'd ever hope to find in a godly male leader. Boaz has a strong reputation as a leader. His subsequent actions prove he is a man of action and a masterful leader, not the kind of man to shirk responsibility or retreat from a challenge. God could easily have chosen to work through men. He chose two women instead.

Two Women and a Baby

The miracle birth of Obed is truly the most joyful moment in the book, hailed by the women who celebrate with Naomi.

This child renews Naomi's life. Instead of the dead end she had reached, Obed creates for Naomi a brand-new opening into the future and a vital new kingdom assignment. No one reading the book of Ruth for the first time would ever anticipate such a remarkable turn of events. The women attribute Naomi's blessings to her foreign-born daughter-in-law with superlative praise. "For your daughter-in-law, who loves you and who is *better to you than seven sons*, has given him birth" (Ruth 4:15, emphasis added). They name the baby Obed, then top off their praise with a punch line: "Naomi has a son!" (4:17).

When Obed is born, the past and the future are joined and all of the loose strands of the story come together. Naomi's sufferings, Ruth's vow, God's mission for each woman, and their true contributions for the kingdom—all unite in one small baby boy, but not in the way you might expect.

Ruth and Naomi each experienced a major turning point long before Obed comes gasping and squalling out of the womb and into their waiting arms. Ruth turned a corner in her life when she refused to abandon Naomi and embraced Naomi's God. Naomi's turning point happened when Ruth unloaded a pile of raw barley at her feet and she realized with astonishment that Yahweh still loved her. These are life-changing moments that dramatically alter both women, for despite their losses and their grief, they derive fresh purpose and meaning from Yahweh's *hesed* and turn outward to sacrifice for others. This is the power of the gospel in their lives.

Obed may change their schedules, daily chores, and sleeping habits. He ends the physical emptiness caused by the absence of sons in the family, for now Elimelech has an heir. But his arrival in this world cannot account for the profound changes that God works in the hearts of the two widows. Obed does not give meaning and purpose to Ruth, for she had both long before he was born. He cannot end Naomi's sufferings, for she will always grieve the losses of her husband and sons. But along with opening up for the two women a window on the future, Obed becomes the beneficiary of all that the two women have gained from what they have suffered and sacrificed. He will carry their past with him into the future.

From the mother who gave him birth, Obed will inherit a caliber of faith in Yahweh that doesn't easily give up, no matter how daunting the obstacles, no matter how impossible the odds. The courageous blood of a risk taker runs through his veins. With a mother like that, it shouldn't surprise anyone to hear of Obed's grandson standing up to a giant warrior armed only with a sling and five small stones.

Obed will also learn a lot about sacrifice from his mother. He will hear about all she has done for Naomi. Word has gotten out about the costly sacrifices Ruth made for her mother-in-law. The women of Bethlehem aren't just spouting overused clichés when they say Ruth is "better than seven sons." They really mean it. Naomi actually is better off with Ruth than a lot of women who gave birth to what the ancient world regarded as the perfect number of sons.

Older women counted on their sons to care for them, to protect them from exploitation and the harsh elements of society, to be their voice, to stand up for their rights, and to preserve their father's name and estate by bringing the next generation of male descendants into the world. Ruth did all of those things for Naomi at great cost to herself and in a culture that tied her hands behind her back, denied her a voice, refused her access to the legal system, and regarded her as useless. It was all uphill for Ruth. But she did it anyway. Not even seven sons would have done as much.

Even with the birth of Obed, Ruth continues sacrificing for Naomi. Anyone would say that after everything Ruth did for Naomi, it was time for her to enjoy a little happiness herself. Marriage to Boaz and the birth of a son seem fitting rewards for such an extraordinary and selfless woman. But Ruth still isn't thinking of herself. She has never veered from her vow.[6] Here at the last, in the final and greatest sacrifice of all, Ruth gives up her child.[7] The story ends, not with a disappointing thud but with a powerful gospel moment.

Naomi gives back too. She isn't a passive spectator of the good things that are happening to Ruth. She isn't Obed's doting grandmother, his babysitter, or his nanny. Naomi is Obed's mother. She will raise him as her own.[8] That's what the women said. "*Naomi has a son!*" (Ruth 4:17, emphasis added). Ruth didn't seek a husband and a baby for herself. Her mission at the threshing floor was on Naomi's behalf. "Boaz was primarily *go'el* to Elimelech. He [Boaz] should accordingly have married Naomi to raise up a child to Elimelech. However, since she was too old Ruth was a substitute and the child in a sense was Naomi's."[9] Ruth served as a surrogate mother for her mother-in-law. The baby she delivered was for Naomi.

But here's the interesting part. Naomi is completely unaware that the whole world is counting on the baby she cradles in her arms for the fulfillment of God's promises to redeem his people and put to rights this fallen world. Obed will not be the last boy born in Bethlehem to hold such a strategic place in the world's history.

Imagine the enormous responsibility of raising such a child. You would want the wise men from the east to come. Summon the teachers of the law, the priests, the rabbis. God chose Naomi to be Obed's teacher. And she is ready for the job, for Naomi has gained wisdom in the school of suffering.

We're still waiting for someone to write the book that will explain all we'd like to know about suffering. We see through a glass darkly now, and nowhere is that more painfully evident to us than when bad things happen and our lives seem to spin wildly out of control. Job and Naomi both ended up with more questions than answers, and so do we. There is mystery to God's ways, and we will never know why he doesn't answer our prayers, stop the blizzards, change the hardened heart, or stop the endless suffering in this world. But from time to time, we do have flashes of clarity, and we have a bit of clarity in Naomi's story.

Naomi would be poorly equipped to do the job of raising the king's grandfather with an untested faith and a shallow knowledge of God that was derived from hearing the Scriptures read in corporate worship and picking up secondhand information about him from other believers. She can't coast on Elimelech's theology either or the teachings of her parents. Vital as all these other resources and influences are, Naomi's participation in kingdom building is seriously impaired if she doesn't know God for herself.

She has to experience him, not just learn *about* him. That means walking with him through storms, adversities, disappointments, and losses. For Naomi, it involved spending time at ground zero—getting angry, feeling betrayed, abandoned, and forgotten. She had to ask the hard questions, cope with unanswered prayers, and endure countless sleepless nights filled with doubts, fears, and anxieties. She had to find God's *hesed* in the middle of the mess. The dark night of the soul is an awful place to be, but that's where God trains his best warriors. Although Naomi looked and felt as if her life was being dismantled and she was being put out of action, God was actually raising her up and equipping her for a mission-critical assignment in his kingdom.

No psalm bears the name Naomi as the lyricist. But traces of her theology are scattered all through the psalms of David, for it is certain that Naomi's influence reached the sweet psalmist of Israel, whose theological roots can be traced through his father, Jesse, to his grandfather, Obed, the child Naomi holds in her arms. Obed learned deep lessons about God at the knee of this female Job. Ellen F. Davis captures the scene:

> The book ends in a way that we do not expect. Boaz and our heroine Ruth are gone from sight, a clear indication that this book is finally something other than a romance. In the end, only the old woman is left, holding the child who is her future and that of her people.[10]

The birth of Obed is a picture of the gospel—suffering and sacrifice, the joy of renewed life, and hope for the future all mingled together. This is the Gospel of Ruth.

THE BLESSED ALLIANCE

Historically, Boaz has been regarded as the romantic lead and true hero of the story. He is the kinsman-redeemer who rescues Ruth from her desperate plight as a childless widow. And while the interpretation we have been considering seems to take a lot of glory away from him (since Ruth initiates the rescue and Boaz joins in as ideas of romance fade into the background), the fact is, he remains a powerful figure in the story and, if anything, only gains strength and stature because of his alliance with Ruth. It is not the outcome anyone would expect.

The relationship between Ruth and Boaz is perhaps the strongest example in the whole Old Testament of how the Blessed Alliance is supposed to work. Two image bearers—male and female—joining forces to advance God's kingdom on earth. Their relationship is rich with wisdom for today, and probably a whole book could be written on the subject. Here are just a few observations to ponder.

First, despite the enormous disparity between them at about every level, their communication flows unhindered. She assesses the situation, formulates ideas, and is unafraid to speak up. He is *interested* in what she has to say—not just being polite and "hearing her out" so she will feel better and leave him alone. He is genuinely interested. Ruth's godly reputation has preceded her, and Boaz listens because he values what she thinks.

Second, Boaz actually learns from Ruth and grows spiritually as a result of her influence. This seems truly backwards. Boaz is the true Israelite, the mature believer, born and raised in the faith. Ruth is an outsider, a recent convert, and the one we'd expect to be doing all the learning. What does she know? Yet Boaz doesn't react defensively to her out-of-the-box suggestions. His male ego, his image, authority, or sense of leadership over his own land—none of these factors gets in his way. He is open to new ideas, even ideas coming from a novice to the faith, a female, and a common gleaner. And he learns from her. In every encounter, Boaz is secure enough to listen, wise enough to act, and humble enough to sacrifice. In their relationship, learning isn't a one-way street. As a result, she opens up to him a whole new dimension of obedience to Yahweh, and Boaz—a truly good man—becomes a better man because of her.

Third, they accomplish more together than either of them could have done separately. Obviously, neither one could conceive a child without the other. But in every other way, their combined efforts achieve results that separately were out of reach.

Without Ruth, Boaz never would have thought of expanding gleaning privileges to her or figuring out an angle to rescue the line of Elimelech. Without Boaz's advocacy, Ruth's efforts to help Naomi would have been severely hampered if not prevented all together. Their relationship underscores the Bible's foundational message about human relationships—namely, that men and women need each other.

Fourth, they are caught up in a purpose that is bigger than the both of them. Their shared passion to live for Yahweh frees them from bogging down over lesser matters and unites them to focus on kingdom issues—like justice, mercy, compassion, *hesed*. They don't keep score—who's doing the most and who's doing the least, who's supposed to lead and who should follow. This releases both to give 100 percent to the task at hand.

In the end, there is deep respect, mutual submission, and a powerful partnership that rocks the community, multiplies *hesed*, and secures the royal line of Christ. Both are making sacrifices. Both are growing stronger. We don't know what happened between them after the birth of Obed, but it's a safe guess that the two of them took up other projects. Boaz was marrying a woman who understood his business from the ground up and wasn't shy about proposing new ideas.

So, does a man become stronger or weaker when he encounters a strong woman like Ruth? Does he pay a price? Is his manhood diminished? Judging from Boaz, it can mean the difference between being a *good* man and becoming a *great* man. Boaz enters the story as a man of valor who deserves our admiration and respect. After joining forces with Ruth, he stands even taller, for he exits as the great-grandfather of King David and a forefather of Jesus.

My Space

Ruth and Naomi answered the question on the jacket of the book my husband bought for me at Blackwell's Bookstore: "Is God good for women?" I don't ask that question any more. He *is* good for us. Better than good—he's *great* for women. He made that point with power in the book of Ruth. His goodness flows steadily to his daughters as we live and breathe, endure sorrows and heartaches, fight battles and partner with our brothers, stumble, fall, and struggle back to our feet in this broken, messed-up, very real world that he is redeeming. He doesn't coddle us, for he wants us to be strong. He takes us through deep waters so we will learn wisdom and know him for ourselves. Our lives are not perfect. We have empty places in our hearts. But we are grounded in the truth that he loves us, and that's what keeps us going. He is changing us. He wants us to change our world.

A rescue effort is underway. Lives are at risk. There's a kingdom to build. A planet to reclaim. God doesn't intend to do any of this without us. He burdens our hearts. He opens our eyes to see faces, needs, and possibilities. He is counting on his daughters to live and proclaim his gospel. Whether we're tucking a child into bed; ministering to a friend; pursuing a heart that is hardened to the gospel; working in the corporate world, the church, and the community; or fighting for justice in some remote region of the earth—God is advancing his kingdom through our efforts and our gifts. And you never know when some small everyday battle you are fighting may turn the tide for the kingdom in a big way.

Now, instead of asking if God is good for women, I'm asking a new question. I stole it from Frances Hodgson Burnett's classic novel, *The Secret Garden*. When the orphaned heroine, Mary Lennox, stumbled over a piece of untended, overgrown land needing to be ruled and subdued, she asked her uncle, "Might I have a bit of earth?"

Sometimes the "bit of earth" we're fighting to rule and subdue is the square foot of ground we're standing on, as we wrestle to trust God when our lives are falling apart and the God-forsaken cry is coming from us. Some battles are for one person—a child, a lost heart, a discouraged friend, a fellow soldier. Sometimes God calls us to fight battles for the men in our lives—our fathers, brothers, husbands, sons, colleagues, and friends. Many of us are awakening to the need to rule and subdue larger territories—to fight for justice and mercy for the widow, the orphan, and the foreigner.

Not every woman has a Boaz in her life. Sometimes the male voices we hear are cautioning us to hold back instead of urging us to serve God wholeheartedly with them. Sometimes the cautioning voices we hear belong to other women. Sometimes those who have the power to facilitate our callings and clear a path for us set up roadblocks instead. Ruth, Naomi, and Boaz remind us powerfully that even in a dark era like the days of the judges, God always has his people and the Blessed Alliance is still alive and well. He is working in our hearts, summoning us to be strong and courageous like Ruth—to embrace and embody his gospel on our "bit of earth."

And God is also working in the hearts of our brothers. He is raising up men—husbands, fathers, brothers, friends, and colleagues—who like Boaz of old are partners in *hesed* and who gladly put their full weight behind what God is doing through his daughters. These strong allies join their sisters in leaving God's fingerprints on the lives of others.

May God bless every woman's life with men like Boaz. But even if there is no Boaz, God is a mighty advocate. God is good for women, and women who know this are strong for his kingdom. God wants to hear his daughters ask, "Might I have a bit of earth?" This is the Gospel of Ruth.

DISCUSSION QUESTIONS

1. If you were traveling with Ruth when she first arrived in Bethlehem, what advice would you give her about how to conduct herself as the newcomer in town?

2. How are lives changed for the better because of Ruth's bold initiatives?

3. How does Ruth speak and act for Yahweh? How are his fingerprints evident through her life?

4. Why does the Cinderella ending create problems for us? Why does this interpretation of the conclusion fail to hold up in the real world? Who gets left out?

5. How does God change the lives of Ruth and Naomi?

6. How is Obed's life blessed by Ruth's passion for Yahweh and Naomi's agonized wrestlings with him?

7. How was God counting on Naomi and Ruth, not just to fight important battles in their immediate circumstances, but by bravely fighting those battles to eventually change the world?

8. How does the story of Ruth and Naomi cast a bigger vision for God's calling on your life today—the call to join his rescue operation for the world? How can you live more courageously for him?

Notes

Introduction : What Women Want to Know

1. Anyone studying or teaching the book of Ruth will want to get their hands on this volume: Robert J. Hubbard Jr., *The Book of Ruth*, New International Commentary on the Old Testament (Grand Rapids: Eerdmans, 1988).

2. Job's story is recorded in the Old Testament book of Job.

3. For further discussion of Eve's forgotten legacy, see Carolyn Custis James, *Lost Women of the Bible: Finding Strength and Significance through Their Stories* (Grand Rapids: Zondervan, 2005), 27–44.

4. Ibid. *Ezer* (pronounced āzer with a long sounding ā, as in razor) is a powerful Hebrew military word that is used most often in the Bible to describe God as Israel's helper. God employs the term twice when he creates the woman. "The LORD God said, 'It is not good for the man to be alone. I will make a helper [*ezer*] suitable for him'" (Genesis 2:18, also 20). The Bible's consistent usage of *ezer* within a military context has led to the conclusion that God created the woman to be a warrior alongside the man in advancing God's kingdom throughout the earth. This is every woman's calling, regardless of her age, marital status, or circumstances. *Every* woman is an *ezer* from birth to death. We are warriors for God's purposes alongside our brothers in Christ. For more on the *ezer*, see also chapter 9 of Carolyn Custis James, *When Life and Beliefs Collide: How Knowing God Makes a Difference* (Grand Rapids: Zondervan, 2001).

5. When God created the man and the woman, "God *blessed* them" (emphasis added) before giving them their mission to "be fruitful and increase in number; fill the earth and subdue it. Rule over the fish of the sea and the birds of the air and over every living creature that moves on the ground" (Genesis 1:28). Men and women are God's A-Team, called to join together as a Blessed Alliance in this global mission to fill the whole earth with worshipers of the living God and to rule the earth as he would—with justice, mercy, righteousness, and peace. For more on the Blessed Alliance, see James, *Lost Women of the Bible*, 37–38.

Chapter One: Looking at God from Ground Zero

1. Eugene Peterson, *A Long Obedience in the Same Direction: Discipleship in an Instant Society* (Downers Grove, IL: InterVarsity Press, 2000), 42.

2. The cycle is explained in Judges 2:10–19. Israel followed their own inclinations. They turned their backs on God and embraced the idols of the people around them, provoking God to anger. He brought judgments, which in turn brought them to repentance. They cried out for his help. He raised up a judge to deliver them from their enemies. They were faithful during the judge's lifetime, but subsequently resumed the cycle, turning away from God to idols. Scholars note that as you make your way through the Old Testament book of Judges, this repeating cycle actually is more of a downward spiral. Conditions worsen. The quality of the judges declines—from Othniel and Deborah, strong judges with courageous faith in God, to Samson, whose faith was mingled with self-indulgence, womanizing, and impetuous actions.

3. Deuteronomy 28:22–24 explains the consequences that would come to Israel as a result of their disobedience, including famine.

4. Cf. Numbers 22–24; Judges 3:12–30.

5. Cf. Genesis 19:30–38. Moab was born to the older daughter of Lot, following the destruction of Sodom and Gomorrah.

6. Cf. Deuteronomy 23:3–6.

7. When the Israelites encamped along the borders of Moab on their way to Canaan, Balak, the king of Moab, attempted to eliminate this threat to his people by paying Balaam to curse them (Numbers 22–24). When this strategy failed, the women of Moab proved more effective, inviting Israelite men to join them in worshiping their gods, an invitation that led to spiritual adultery and sexual immorality. This breech in Israel's loyalty to God introduced a far greater peril to Israel than King Balak could have ever hoped, namely, the fierce wrath of God against his own people (Numbers 25:1–9). King Solomon's marriages to Moabite women provide another tragic example. See 1 Kings 11:1–13, esp. 1, 2, 7–9.

8. Elie Wiesel, *Night* (New York: Hill and Wang, 2006), 32.

9. In the ancient Hebrew culture, a woman was bound to her husband's family even after his death. "A widow could return to her family only if her purchase price was repaid to her husband's heirs." Bonnie Bowman Thurston, *Widows: A Woman's Ministry in the Early Church* (Minneapolis: Fortress, 1989), 13.

10. The main theme of Ruth 1 is the idea of returning. The narrator repeats the Hebrew word *shub* (pronounced "shoob") again and again to make that point. Naomi *returns* to Bethlehem (v.7). She instructs her daughters-in-law to *go back*, or *return*, to Moab (v.8). The word *shub* occurs repeatedly throughout the chapter—vv. 6, 7, 8, 10, 11, 12, 15 (twice), 16, 22 (twice). It also appears in 2:6 and 4:3. In our English versions of the Bible, it is translated in a variety of ways, so it's easy for us to miss this emphasis.

11. See also the words of Jeremiah, "He drew his bow and made me the target for his arrows. He pierced my heart with arrows from his quiver" (Lamentations 3:12–13).

12. This is the translation given by Robert J. Hubbard Jr., *The Book of Ruth*, New International Commentary on the Old Testament (Grand Rapids: Eerdmans, 1988).

13. "The vague *Thus* reflects the formula's ultimate origin in ceremonies which solemnized ancient treaties and covenants. As the oath was

pronounced, symbolic actions (cf., e.g., the modern gesture of slashing one's finger across the throat) alluded to the slaughter of animals, an earlier part of the ceremony, and invoked a similar fate for breach of promise by the speaker. Thus, Ruth voluntarily took on dire, unspecified consequences if the condition next stipulated happened. Given Naomi's testimony against Yahweh (v. 13; cf. vv. 20–21), Ruth could conceivably expect the worst" (Hubbard, *The Book of Ruth*, 119).

14. C. S. Lewis, *Surprised by Joy: The Shape of My Early Life* (New York: Harcourt Brace & Company, 1955), 216–17.

15. There's no indication that when Mahlon and Ruth married, she embraced his faith in Yahweh. Some have argued that she was converted to Yahweh before this incident on the road, based on Naomi's statement thanking Ruth for her loyal love [*hesed*] in Moab (Ruth 1:8). However, this statement also includes Orpah, and certainly we have all encountered nonbelievers who expressed the extraordinary kindnesses attributed to Ruth and Orpah. Furthermore, Naomi's counsel to return to their people and their gods implies that neither daughter-in-law had at this point in time embraced faith in Yahweh.

CHAPTER TWO: LEFT BEHIND — A WOMAN ON HER OWN

1. First Union National Bank — Seminar for Women, 2000, sponsored by Lowndes, Drosdick, Doster, Kantor & Reed, P.A., Attorneys at Law (Statistics from the U.S. Census Bureau).

2. Patricia Carrington, Julia Collins, Claudia Gerbasi, and Ann Haynes, *Love You, Mean It: A True Story of Love, Loss, and Friendship* (New York: Hyperion, 2006).

3. Naomi uses legal language that "portrays her as a defendant in a legal action who has already been found guilty and punished (i.e., her misfortune) but who knows neither the charges nor the testimony against her" (Robert J. Hubbard Jr., *The Book of Ruth*, New International Commentary on the Old Testament [Grand Rapids: Eerdmans, 1988], 127).

   Naomi: "Yahweh *has testified against me*, and Shaddai has heaped all this trouble on me!" (Ruth 1:21, Hubbard translation, emphasis added).

   Job: "As surely as God lives, who *has denied me justice*, the Almighty, who has made me taste bitterness of soul, as long as I have life within me, the breath of God in my nostrils, my lips will not speak wickedness, and my tongue will utter no deceit" (Job 27:2–4, emphasis added).

4. Naomi's sudden appearance stirred up the women of Bethlehem. There was a great disturbance in the village. Some element of confusion is implied, an excitement with some degree of distress. Cf. R. Laird Harris, Gleason L. Archer Jr., Bruce K. Waltke, eds, *Theological Word Book of the Old Testament* (Chicago: Moody Bible Institute, 1980), 1:212–13.

5. Katharine Doob Sakenfeld, *Ruth*, Interpretation: A Bible Commentary for Teaching and Preaching (Louisville: John Knox, 1999), 35.

6. Exodus 15:20; Micah 6:4.

7. Bonnie Bowman Thurston, *The Widows: A Women's Ministry in the Early Church* (Minneapolis: Fortress, 1989), 9.
8. William Dalrymple, "The Outcasts," *The Sunday Times Magazine,* August 16, 1992, 16–24.
9. Ibid., 20–22.
10. Ibid., 22.
11. Ibid., 24.
12. Thurston, *The Widow,* 25, commenting on Luke 7:11–17.
13. "Do not take advantage of a widow or an orphan. If you do and they cry out to me, I will certainly hear their cry. My anger will be aroused, and I will kill you with the sword; your wives will become widows and your children fatherless" (Exodus 22:23–24). See also Deuteronomy 27:19; Psalm 146:9. One of Job's friends falsely accused him of mistreating widows, thinking that this is what explained Job's sufferings (Job 22:9; cf. 29:13).
14. Isaiah 1:17, 23; 10:1–2; Jeremiah 7:5–7; 22:3; Ezekiel 22:7; Zechariah 7:9–10; Malachi 3:5. The widow was a reliable indicator of how well God's people recalled what God had done for them when they were helpless slaves in Egypt (Deuteronomy 24:17–22).
15. Thurston, *The Widow,* 13–14. According to Thurston, "In the Old Testament, the widow's lot was so unhappy and piteous that undue severity against her was prohibited and, along with strangers, orphans, and the poor, she was commended to the charity of the people." Cf. Deuteronomy 10:18–19; 14:28–29; 16:10–15; 24:17–18; 27:19.
16. 1 Kings 17:7–16.
17. Luke 21:1–3.
18. Ruth A. Tucker and Walter Liefeld, *Daughters of the Church: Women and Ministry from New Testament Times to the Present* (Grand Rapids: Zondervan, 1987), 31.
19. Acts 6:1–7; 9:36–43.
20. Thurston, *The Widow,* 54.
21. Ibid.
22. Luke 18:1–8.
23. Thurston, *The Widow,* 25.
24. See Matthew 1:1–17, esp. v. 5.

CHAPTER THREE: WISDOM GLEANED FROM EMPTY ARMS

1. According to Genesis 25:20, 26, Isaac was forty when he married Rebekah and sixty when she finally gave birth to their twin sons, Esau and Jacob.
2. In Genesis 16:2, Sarah laments, "The LORD has kept me from having children." See also Genesis 20:18 (women in King Abimelech's household); 29:31 (Leah); 30:22 (Rachel); 1 Samuel 1:5–6 (Hannah). In Deuteronomy 7:13; 28:4, 11, 18; and 30:9, God asserts his lordship over the womb.
3. Nicholas Wolterstorff, *Lament for a Son* (Grand Rapids: Eerdmans, 1987), 69.
4. Ibid., 26.

5. Philip Yancey, *Prayer: Does It Make Any Difference?* (Grand Rapids: Zondervan, 2006), 37.
6. Romans 4:18–25.
7. To the Romans, Paul announced a gospel of power. "I am not ashamed of the gospel, because it is the power of God for the salvation of everyone who believes: first for the Jew, then for the Gentile" (Romans 1:16). He wrote to the church in Ephesus, "You were dead in your transgressions and sins.... But because of his great love for us, God, who is rich in mercy, made us alive with Christ even when we were dead.... And God raised us up with Christ" (Ephesians 2:1, 4–6).

CHAPTER FOUR: BREAKING THE RULES IN BETHLEHEM

1. Paul Halsall, "Sojourner Truth: 'Ain't I a Woman?' December 1851," *Modern History Sourcebook*, August 1997, available at http://www.fordham.edu/halsall/mod/sojtruth-woman.html.
2. Scholars are divided over whether Ruth is *announcing* her decision to glean to Naomi or if she is *asking* for Naomi's permission as the NIV translation suggests, "*Let me go* to the fields and pick up the leftover grain" (Ruth 2:2, emphasis added). Both Robert J. Hubbard Jr. (*The Book of Ruth*, New International Commentary on the Old Testament [Grand Rapids: Eerdmans, 1988], 136) and Edward F. Campbell Jr. (*Ruth*, Anchor Bible [Garden City, NY: Doubleday, 1975], 91–92) believe Ruth is stating her intention. Katherine Doob Sakenfeld writes, "The Hebrew construction suggests more a statement of intention than a request for permission, although Naomi's reply suggests that she gives consent" (*Ruth*, Interpretation: A Bible Commentary for Teaching and Preaching [Louisville: John Knox, 1999], 39).

    Considering Ruth's consistent pattern of decisive behavior (which the full narrative establishes), I am inclined to think that Ruth is stating her intention. Furthermore, at this particular stage, Naomi is in no frame of mind to enter into this decision. Clearly, Ruth is assuming responsibility for their welfare and taking the initiative by volunteering to do a distasteful and dangerous job. At the same time, she is not pushy or disrespectful, but honors Naomi by presenting her plan. She perfectly balances a strong resolve to do whatever it takes to care for Naomi with a deep regard for those with whom she is dealing. The decision to glean is difficult because risk is involved. Yet gleaning is necessary for their survival; Ruth really has no choice.
3. Philip Yancey, *Disappointment with God* (Grand Rapids: Zondervan, 1992), 236.
4. The NIV translates this phrase as "man of standing," but the Hebrew terms are actually much stronger, indicating both might and valor.
5. Sakenfeld, *Ruth*, 38.
6. R. Laird Harris, Gleason L. Archer Jr., Bruce K. Waltke, eds., *Theological Word Book of the Old Testament* (Chicago: Moody Bible Institute, 1980), 1:271–72.
7. Even his name speaks well of him and reflects his ability to help. Boaz means "in him is strength."

8. Hubbard, *The Book of Ruth*, 135.
9. The book of Ruth describes the relationship between Boaz and Elimelech in two different ways. In Ruth 2:1 and 3:2, Boaz is described as a "relative" or "kinsman," which is more of a general description of their relationship. Simply put, they are related. In Ruth 2:20; 3:9, 12, Boaz is referred to as a *go'el*, or kinsman-redeemer, a family relationship that came with major obligations to assist sacrificially a relative who had come into misfortune.
10. "When you reap the harvest of your land, do not reap to the very edges of your field or gather the gleanings of your harvest. Do not go over your vineyard a second time or pick up the grapes that have fallen. Leave them for the poor and the alien. I am the LORD your God" (Leviticus 19:9–10).

    "When you are harvesting your crops and forget to bring in a bundle of grain from your field, don't go back to get it. Leave it for the foreigners, orphans, and widows. Then the LORD your God will bless you in all you do. When you beat the olives from your olive trees, don't go over the boughs twice. Leave some of the olives for the foreigners, orphans, and widows. When you gather the grapes in your vineyard, don't glean the vines after they are picked. Leave the remaining grapes for the foreigners, orphans, and widows. Remember that you were slaves in the land of Egypt. That is why I am giving you this command" (Deuteronomy 24:19–22, NLT).

    Landowners were on their honor to comply. By complying, they acknowledged Yahweh as the true landowner and themselves as stewards of his property. By showing mercy to the poor they were also remembering (and imitating) Yahweh's mercy on them when they were helpless slaves in Egypt. When Ruth went to glean, she tapped into the ancient Israelite welfare system, which gave the poor a way to provide for themselves with dignity by working with their own hands.
11. Hubbard, *The Book of Ruth*, 136. "Unfortunately, greedy owners and reapers probably often obstructed the efforts of gleaners by ridicule, tricks, and in some cases outright expulsion."
12. Cf. Ruth 2:13.
13. Frederick Bush, *Ruth/Esther*, Word Biblical Commentary 9 (Waco, TX: Word, 1996), 113.
14. Hubbard, *The Book of Ruth*, 150.
15. Ibid., 161.
16. Ibid., 156.

CHAPTER FIVE: THE POWER OF *HESED*

1. Augustine, *Confessions: Books I-XIII*, trans. F. J. Sheed (Indianapolis: Hackett, 1993), 56.
2. Ibid.
3. "While ancient Jewish and modern commentators speculate about the deaths of the men for disobedience in going to Moab or marrying Moabites, the story that we receive gives no attention to God's relationship to Elimelech, Mahlon, and Chilion. Nor does the narrator claim that God had turned against Naomi. That is her perception, expressed in her speech. Unlike Job, she is not portrayed as being

interested in why calamity has struck. Unlike those psalmists who uttered prayers of lament, she is not portrayed as asking God for a change in her condition; indeed, given the nature of her problem, a prayer for redress would not have been readily imaginable. Her spirit has been crushed even beyond the point of prayer. Yet as events unfold by the end of the story, the prayer not uttered because it could not even be imagined will nonetheless receive its answer." Katharine Doob Sakenfeld, *Ruth*, Interpretation: A Bible Commentary for Teaching and Preaching (Louisville: John Knox, 1999), 29.

4. Ibid., 36.
5. Robert J. Hubbard Jr., *The Book of Ruth*, New International Commentary on the Old Testament (Grand Rapids: Eerdmans, 1988), 179.
6. Ibid., 179.
7. Ibid., 181.
8. Sakenfeld, *Ruth*, 11–12.
9. "*Hesed* is regularly used as object of the verb 'to do'; hence the focus is on *an act of hesed* or loyalty" (emphasis in original; Katherine Doob Sakenfeld, "Loyalty and Love: The Language of Human Interconnections in the Hebrew Bible," *Backgrounds for the Bible*, ed. Michael Patrick O'Connor and David Noel Freedman [Winona Lake, IN: Eisenbrauns, 1987], 221).

CHAPTER SIX: FINDING GOD'S FINGERPRINTS ON OUR LIVES

1. Stanley J. Grenz, *Theology for the Community of God* (Nashville: Broadman & Holman, 1994), 129.
2. Frank A. James III, *Peter Martyr Vermigli and Predestination: The Augustinian Inheritance of an Italian Reformer* (Oxford: Clarendon, 1998), 202–3.
3. Naomi prays for Orpah and Ruth (Ruth 1:8–9). Boaz and his workers seek God's presence and his blessing for each other (2:4). In his encounters with Ruth, Boaz twice is moved to pray that God will reward her for the enormous sacrifices she is making for Naomi (2:12; 3:10). Naomi asks Yahweh to bless Boaz for his *hesed* in the barley field. The structure of the sentence has long puzzled Old Testament scholars who cannot determine for sure if she's talking about Yahweh's *hesed* or Boaz's. I'm inclined to believe the two are so intertwined, she really does mean both. "The LORD bless him! *He* has not stopped showing his kindness [*hesed*] to the living and the dead" (2:20, emphasis added). The book concludes with Bethlehem elders and villagers seeking God's blessings on Boaz and Ruth (4:11–12) and women praising God with Naomi for the birth of Obed (4:14).
4. Eugene Peterson, *A Long Obedience in the Same Direction: Discipleship in an Instant Society* (Downers Grove, IL: InterVarsity Press, 2000), 138.
5. Rick Warren, *The Purpose Driven Life: What on Earth Am I Here For?* (Grand Rapids: Zondervan, 2002), 275.
6. Grenz, *Theology for the Community of God*, 160.

1. Maeve Binchy, "Telling Stories," in a collection of short stories entitled *Telling Stories* (London: Hodder & Stoughton, 1992).
2. "The span would run roughly from late April to the beginning of June," according to Edward F. Campbell Jr., *Ruth*, Anchor Bible (Garden City, NY: Doubleday, 1975), 108.
3. Katharine Sakenfeld accounts for why Boaz is winnowing barley (which was harvested earlier) by pointing to practices in today's Middle East, where harvesters have "techniques for sealing the early harvest against weather, insects, and rodents for a number of weeks until the work schedule permits attention to threshing and winnowing" (Katharine Doob Sakenfeld, *Ruth*, Interpretation: A Bible Commentary for Teaching and Preaching [Louisville: John Knox, 1999], 52).
4. Threshing floors were often known for drunkenness and immorality.
5. Harvested grain was carted to the threshing floor, where stalks were laid out and trampled under animals hooves or crushed under cart wheels or threshing sledges made of planks embedded with sharp stones or pieces of metal. Individuals processing smaller amounts of grain (such as a gleaner would gather) would beat the grain with a stick or flail. Such threshing removed the husks from the kernels.

    Winnowing followed; harvesters used shovels or forks to toss the threshed grain up in the air where the wind would blow the "chaff" or the straw pieces away and the heavier grain would fall back to the earth (cf. Psalm 1:4). See H. N. Richardson, "Threshing," *The Interpreter's Dictionary of the Bible*, ed. George Arthur Buttrick (Nashville: Abingdon, 1962), 4:636.
6. Archeologists tell us that threshing floors were usually situated outside the city gates—close enough to the city to facilitate transporting threshed grain inside, but far enough from the walls to take the best advantage of the prevailing breezes.
7. Frederick Bush, *Ruth/Esther*, Word Biblical Commentary 9 (Waco, TX: Word, 1996), 155.
8. Daniel I. Block, *Judges, Ruth*, New American Commentary 6 (Nashville: Broadman & Holman, 1999), 609–10.
9. Campbell, *Ruth*, 131. The Hebrew word for "feet" can also mean legs and, according to Campbell, "comes from a word that is a standard euphemism for the sexual organs." The words for "uncover" and "wing" (Ruth 3:9) in other contexts refer to sexual intercourse (cf. Deuteronomy 22:30 and 27:20 in NASB or NKJV). Campbell further notes that forms of other words, such as "know" (Ruth 3:3, 10, 14, 18) and "to lie down" (used eight times in 3:4–14), also contribute to a mood of sexual tension, for in other contexts familiar to Hebrew readers these words connote sexual intercourse.
10. Campbell, *Ruth*, 132.
11. Bush (*Ruth/Esther*, 222) writes regarding Levirate marriage, "the marriage is effected by its consummation; no ceremony is necessary." And while it doesn't appear that Naomi had Levirate marriage in mind, but believed that option didn't exist (cf. Ruth 1:11–13), she seems to have

expected Ruth to return to her a married woman. Her question, upon Ruth's return home in the morning, "How did it go?" seems to imply that expectation. This fits also with the irregularities of this marriage arrangement: no formal marriage negotiations and no bride price or dowry. There will be no fanfare or marriage celebration. He can take her now, or not. The fact that legal issues become involved and someone exists with greater rights to Elimelech's estate than Boaz throw a wrench in Naomi's plan and cause Boaz to exercise restraint.

12. Adele Berlin, *Poetics and Interpretation of Biblical Narrative* (Winona Lake, IN: Eisenbrauns, 1994), 90.

13. Levirate law: "If brothers are living together and one of them dies without a son, his widow must not marry outside the family. Her husband's brother shall take her and marry her and fulfill the duty of a brother-in-law to her. The first son she bears shall carry on the name of the dead brother so that his name will not be blotted out from Israel. However, if a man does not want to marry his brother's wife, she shall go to the elders at the town gate and say, 'My husband's brother refuses to carry on his brother's name in Israel. He will not fulfill the duty of a brother-in-law to me.' Then the elders of his town shall summon him and talk to him. If he persists in saying, 'I do not want to marry her,' his brother's widow shall go up to him in the presence of the elders, take off one of his sandals, spit in his face and say, 'This is what is done to the man who will not build up his brother's family line' " (Deuteronomy 25:5–9).

14. Kinsman-redeemer law: "If any of your Israelite relatives go bankrupt and are forced to sell some inherited land, then a close relative, a kinsman redeemer, may buy it back for them." (Leviticus 25:25, NLT).

15. The price of a field was calculated by the number of harvests until the Year of Jubilee—a national celebration every fifty years where the land would automatically revert to the original owner. So a man could be paying for one year's harvest or fifty, depending on where they were on the nation's calendar (cf. Leviticus 25:23–31).

16. Naomi in 1:11, 12, 13; 2:2, 22; 3:1; Boaz in 2:8; 3:10, 11.

17. Geraldine Brooks, *Nine Parts of Desire: The Hidden World of Islamic Women* (New York: Anchor, 1996), 67.

18. R. Laird Harris, Gleason L. Archer Jr., Bruce K. Waltke, eds., *Theological Word Book of the Old Testament* (Chicago: Moody Bible Institute, 1980), 1:271–72.

19. Significantly, the Hebrew Bible places the book of Ruth among the wisdom writings immediately following Proverbs, as if to say, after Proverbs 31, "Now here in Ruth is an example of a noble [*hayil*] woman." The application of *hayil* to Boaz, Ruth, and the Proverbs 31 woman is reason enough for us to upgrade our interpretations of the Proverbs 31 woman, for she too is a woman of courageous valor. For further discussion, see Carolyn Custis James, *When Life and Beliefs Collide* (Grand Rapids: Zondervan, 2001), 187.

20. Ibid.

21. Bush, *Ruth/Esther*, 178.

Chapter Eight: The Three Faces of Submission

1. Jay G. Silverman, Anita Raj, Lorelei A. Mucci, and Jeanne E. Hathaway, "Dating Violence against Adolescent Girls and Associated Substance Use, Unhealthy Weight Control, Sexual Risk Behavior, Pregnancy, and Suicidality," *Journal of the American Medical Association* 286/5 (2001): 572–79.
2. "Hope for the Girl Child: A Briefing Paper to the United Nations Commission on the Status of Women at Its 51st Session" (Monrovia, CA: World Vision International, Gender and Development Department and World Vision International Policy and Advocacy, 2007), 8.
3. "For I have come down from heaven not to do my will but to do the will of him who sent me" (John 6:38).
4. "No one takes [my life] from me, but I lay it down of my own accord" (John 10:18).
5. Robert J. Hubbard Jr., *The Book of Ruth*, New International Commentary on the Old Testament (Grand Rapids: Eerdmans, 1988), 212.
6. Ibid., 213.
7. Eugene H. Peterson, *Run with the Horses: The Quest for Life at Its Best* (Downers Grove, IL: InterVarsity Press, 1983), 43.
8. Lisa Graham McMinn, *Growing Strong Daughters: Encouraging Girls to Become All They're Meant to Be* (Grand Rapids: Baker, 2000).

Chapter Nine: When Women Initiate and Men Respond

1. See for example, "Her husband is respected at the city gate, where he takes his seat among the elders of the land.... Give her the reward she has earned, and let her works bring her praise at the city gate" (Proverbs 31:23, 31).
2. Scholars debate what may have happened to Elimelech's land before (or after) his departure for Moab. Under normal circumstances, when a man went bankrupt, he put his property up for sale. It is possible that Elimelech sold his land to an outsider. However, given the fact that Bethlehem was under a famine, his land was hardly prime property, and it's hard to imagine him finding a buyer. This is one of many options, and I refer you to the commentaries for a thorough treatment of this discussion.

   The narrator offers no explanation, which means that for us to understand the message of the book, this detail isn't necessary. For purposes of this discussion, however, I'm following the theory that Elimelech's famine-stricken land had lain dormant all these years and that, because his kinsmen were suffering from the same prolonged famine conditions, none of them had been in a position to help him out ... until now.
3. Numbers 27:1–11; 36:1–13; Joshua 17:3–6 document the ground breaking case of the daughters of Zelophehad, who inherited their father's property.

4. Genealogies in the Bible often have gaps—places where names and generations are intentionally omitted or the list is telescoped to include only the main names and also to position certain names strategically in the list. For example, the fifth name (Nahshon in this list) is significant, but not as significant as the seventh, Boaz (see Robert J. Hubbard Jr., *The Book of Ruth*, New International Commentary on the Old Testament [Grand Rapids: Eerdmans, 1988], 283). Scholars suspect gaps between Nahshon and Salmon and/or between Salmon and Boaz, but for our purposes here, we are discussing the names without regard to the existence of gaps.

5. Numbers 2:3–9; 10:12–14.

6. Numbers 7:12–17.

7. The narrator interrupts his story to explain this ancient custom to his initial readers. These were people living *at least* three or four generations later, during the reign of David or Solomon. "(Now in earlier times in Israel, for the redemption and transfer of property to become final, one party took off his sandal and gave it to the other. This was the method of legalizing transactions in Israel.) So the kinsman-redeemer said to Boaz, 'Buy it yourself.' And he removed his sandal" (Ruth 4:7–8). Already this ritual for ratifying the transfer of property from one man to another had fallen out of practice and needed explaining. We are even further removed from this tradition and are left to guess at the significance of a sandal.

Scholars devote lengthy passages to possible meanings of this symbolic act. They even debate which man is removing his sandal and giving it to the other, although the consensus is that the nearer kinsman's sandal is involved. We will never know for sure the precise meaning of the passing of a sandal. What is certain is that Bethlehemites were witnessing the transfer of redemption rights from Mr. No-Name to Boaz, and the sandal ceremony served as documentation.

Chapter Ten: Good to Great

1. For a fuller treatment of Tamar's story, see Carolyn Custis James, *Lost Women of the Bible: Finding Strength and Significance through Their Stories* (Grand Rapids: Zondervan, 2005), 102–19.

2. Matthew's gospel identifies Boaz's mother as a foreigner—Rahab the Canaanite from Jericho (see Matthew 1:5). His father descended from Perez, whose mother was also Gentile. According to the math, this means Boaz was *more than half* Gentile. With the birth of Obed, the royal line of Jesus is at least three-fourths Gentile. This is another way the book of Ruth reflects the richness of the gospel.

3. Cf. Matthew 1:3–6.

4. Jack M. Sasson, *Ruth: A New Translation with a Philological Commentary and a Formalist-Folklorist Interpretation* (Baltimore: Johns Hopkins University Press, 1979), 171–72.

5. Katharine Doob Sakenfeld, *Ruth*, Interpretation: A Bible Commentary for Teaching and Preaching (Louisville: John Knox, 1999), 87.

6. Some scholars believe that Ruth left Naomi to live with Boaz. But this can hardly be the case, for Ruth's vow "where you lodge I will lodge" did not carry the condition that this promise was only good so long as Ruth never received a better offer. However they worked it out, I'm firmly convinced that Ruth never left Naomi.

7. Ruth's gift of Obed to Naomi is the final piece of evidence to support the theory that when Ruth proposed marriage to Boaz, she wasn't seeking security for herself. Rather, she was volunteering as a surrogate mother for Naomi, the widow to whom the Levirate Law would have applied if she hadn't been postmenopausal. Ruth is offering herself—barrenness notwithstanding—to conceive and bear a child to replace the sons Naomi has lost.

8. According to levirate practices, Obed will carry on Elimelech's name and is legally regarded as the son of Elimelech and Naomi. Designated as Naomi's son, he comes under her care and guardianship. Certainly in his early formative years (when a young child was under his mother's care), Naomi would be the major influence on the young Obed.

9. Leon Morris, *Ruth: An Introduction and Commentary*, Tyndale Old Testament Commentary (London: Tyndale, 1968), 315.

10. Ellen F. Davis and Margaret Adams Parker, *Who Are You, My Daughter?—Reading Ruth through Image and Text* (Louisville: Westminster John Knox, 2003), 117.

Lost Women of the Bible
The Women We Thought We Knew

Carolyn Custis James

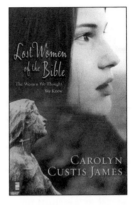

You know the women of the Bible, but you don't know them like this...

It's easy for Christian women—young and old—to get lost between the opportunities and demands of the present and the biblical teachings of the past. They live in a confusing world, caught in the crossfire between church and culture. Although home and family still remain central, more women than ever, by choice or by necessity, are blending home, career, and ministry. They need strong biblical role models to help them meet these challenges.

Building on solid scholarship and a determination to wrestle honestly with perplexing questions, author Carolyn Custis James sheds new light on ancient stories that bring the women of the Bible into the twenty-first century. This fresh look at the women in the Bible unearths surprising new insights and a powerful message that will leave readers feeling challenged, encouraged, and deeply valued.

Rediscover and be inspired by:
- Eve
- Sarah
- Hagar
- Tamar
- Hannah
- Esther
- Mary
- and others

Available in stores and online!

ZONDERVAN®
.com

When Life and Beliefs Collide
How Knowing God Makes a Difference

Carolyn Custis James

Sooner or later, life's difficulties bring every Christian woman to God's doorstep with questions too personal to ignore. "Why does God let me go through such painful circumstances?" "Why does he seem indifferent to my prayers?" We're tired of spiritual pie in the sky. We want authentic, God-as-he-really-is faith—the kind that holds us together when our world is falling apart and equips us to offer strength and hope to others.

When Life and Beliefs Collide raises a long-overdue call for us to think seriously about what we believe about God. With passion, brilliance, and eloquence, Carolyn Custis James weaves stories of contemporary women with episodes from the life of Mary of Bethany to illustrate the practical benefits of knowing God deeply. Examining the misperceptions and abuses that discourage women from pursuing a deeper understanding of God, this insightful book demonstrates how practical and down to earth knowing God can be.

"This outstanding book offers the best demonstration that everyone needs theology, the best expository account of Mary and Martha, and the best trajectory for women's ministry in modern North America that I have yet read." —James I. Packer

"Thoughtful, scholarly, and motivating . . . should inspire and encourage women for years to come." —Joni Eareckson Tada

"You will not think the same way, nor hopefully be the same, after reading this thought-provoking book." —Vonette Zachary Bright

". . . affirms women in their calling, chosen-ness, and gifting, and makes us know we are cherished and planned for." —Jill Briscoe

Available in stores and online!

ZONDERVAN®
.com